GETTING STARTED IN
RADIO CONTROL
AIRPLANES

by GERRY YARRISH

From the Publishers of

MODEL
Airplane
NEWS

About the Author

Introduced to R/C aviation at an early age by his father, Gerry Yarrish is an accomplished model designer and builder and a self-taught flier. He and his father crashed and rebuilt many airplanes until they got it right! When they one day returned home from the local schoolyard with a model that was still intact, it was a great accomplishment.

From 1975 to 1979, Gerry served in the U.S. Air Force, but his tour of duty didn't interrupt his modeling: he continued to build and fly R/C airplanes.

In 1990, Gerry joined Air Age Publishing as associate editor, and he has written more than 160 R/C-related magazine articles. Since 1995, he has been an editor of *Model Airplane News magazine*, and he is the executive editor of *Radio Control Boat Modeler*.

Gerry also found the time to build and fly an all-wood homebuilt ultralight aircraft, and he is a master scuba diver and dive master with more than 500 dives in his logbook.

With his wife, Anita, and 8-year-old daughter, Rebecca Janelle, Gerry lives in New Milford, Connecticut, in a log cabin that he and Anita built themselves. Rebecca thinks it's perfectly normal to go to the flying field with her dad and play with her little friends while dad plays with his big friends and flies his planes.

Acknowledgments and Dedication

Edward Carl Yarrish, circa 1952.

I only *wrote* this book; a lot of people made it possible, and all of them deserve my thanks.

My mom, Melieta, encouraged me always to do my best, and she didn't get too mad at me when I irked the English teacher by reading model airplane magazines in class. My wife, Anita, convinced me I should pursue a career in publishing and was my first "editor." My many "R/C friends" taught me a lot (and I stole many ideas from them, too!).

My thanks also go to shop owner Craig Trachten and the rest of the gang at Hobby Town USA in New Milford, Connecticut; they lent the use of several of the products and planes that are featured in this book.

But most especially, I dedicate this book to my father, Edward Carl Yarrish, who introduced me to this wonderful, lifelong hobby. He is no longer with us but is still a huge influence. Thanks, Dad!

■ **Group Editor-in-Chief/Technical Editor** Tom Atwood
■ **Copy Director** Lynne Sewell ■ **Senior Copy Editor** Molly O'Byrne
■ **Copy Editor** Corey Weber
■ **Corporate Art Director** Betty Nero ■ **Graphic Designer** Stephanie Fagan
■ **Staff Photographer** Walter Sidas
■ **Technical Illustrations** Jim Newman, Mark B. Rittinger, Gerry Yarrish
■ **Director of Operations** David Bowers
■ **Production Associates** Chris Hoffmeister, Tom Hurley
■ **Director of Circulation** Ned Bixler ■ **Circulation Assistant** P.J. Uva

AirAGE

www.airage.com

Published by Air Age Inc., 100 East Ridge, Ridgefield, CT 06977; (203) 431-9000; fax (203) 431-3000; www.airage.com.

PRINTED IN THE USA

Table of Contents

Introduction

Starting any new hobby involves taking that first unsure step. Like many other leisure-time activities, radio control (R/C) model airplane building and flying offer many directions in which you may go exploring. I hope that reading this book will

smooth your path into R/C and will give you a solid foundation on which to build a rewarding and enjoyable pastime. Where I recommend R/C organizations, publications, or products, you'll find the addresses and other contact information toward the end of the book.

If you have chosen R/C model airplanes as a hobby, you are probably interested in aviation in general; for many of us, our R/C activities help us fulfill our dreams to be pilots—one with his feet planted firmly on the ground while the aircraft zooms overhead, but a pilot nevertheless.

Perhaps you like to build with your hands and take great pride in what you create. Building a model airplane and then flying it is a wonderful way to express your creativity.

Or maybe deep down inside, you fancy yourself as a fighter pilot or an aerobatic daredevil, and you long to be released from your earthly bonds. R/C model airplanes can make daydreams come true.

Welcome to R/C airplanes. Now get ready to have some serious fun.

Gerry Yarrish

Getting Started

Whatever has caught your fancy about R/C airplanes, you have two enjoyable challenges to look forward to: building (or just "final assembling," if you buy a built kit) and then learning how to fly your creation. Where do you start? Go to the newsstand, the nearest hobby shop, or a large bookstore, and pick up some of the model airplane magazines published every month. *Model Airplane News* is a great source of information on what's going on in the world of R/C. Read the articles and see what interests you, then, if you haven't already done so, head to a hobby shop.

Your local hobby shop is the place to go. You'll find a wealth of information there. In most cases, you'll find that the store's owner is a serious R/C'er and able to help you get off to a good start.

Look for a hobby shop that specializes in R/C models. There, you'll find the products and accessories you'll need to build your first model. Get to know the shop owner; he's likely to be an R/C enthusiast himself. Ask whether there's a local club and a place to fly your model. Ahh ...! The flying field! That's where you can socialize with other modelers and have some real fun putting your model through its paces. If you already have a friend in the hobby, you're ahead of the game; if you don't, soon after you join a flying club, you will.

Next, join the Academy of Model Aeronautics (AMA). Before you're allowed to fly at a club's site, AMA membership is usually required; it provides insurance coverage and publishes a monthly magazine (*Model Aviation*) that contains useful information on events and contests throughout the USA. You'll find information on the AMA at the hobby shop and your local club, and its address is listed at the back of this book (see Appendix 2, "Useful addresses and websites"). The Sport Flyers of America organization also offers insurance for R/C modelers. Whichever organization you choose, getting your membership card is an important step toward becoming an R/C pilot.

Now let's build that first

Join the Academy of Model Aeronautics or the Sport Flyers of America. As a card-carrying member of one of these organizations, you'll have insurance protection when you fly your model.

airplane. It isn't all that hard; in fact, many find the building as much fun as flying. First, let's learn some of the terminology.

Powered by a .25-size, 2-stroke glow engine and shown here in stable, straight and level flight, the Nifty Fifty made by the Florio Flyer Corp. is a good 3-channel trainer.

Figure 1 Basic model airplane parts.

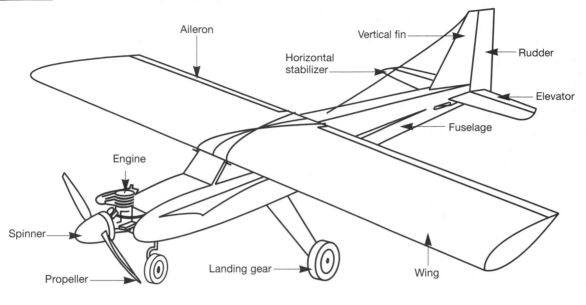

AIRCRAFT TERMINOLOGY

Before we get into the popular types of beginner model airplanes, let's go to ground school and talk about a model airplane's basic parts. The terms used to identify the parts of a model are exactly the same as for a full-size aircraft (See Figure 1). The three main parts are the fuselage, the wing and the tail components.

■ **FUSELAGE.** The fuselage (or "fuse" in model-speak!) is the model's main body—the structure to which all other components are attached; it houses the radio and, typically, the powerplant (motor and batteries or engine and fuel tank). Most trainers, and many scale and sport models, have a box-type fuselage construction—four flat sides: a top and a bottom and two vertical sides. A box construction offers the easiest way to build a strong, simple fuselage, and it has the bonus of being easy to cover and finish. Most of the models in this book feature simple, box-fuselage construction.

Figure 2 Main fuselage parts.

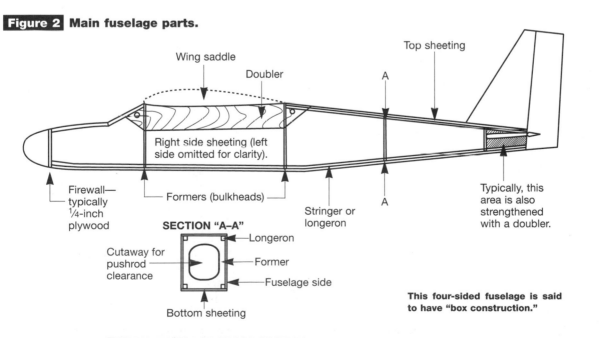

TYPICAL FUSELAGE CROSS-SECTION

Figure 3 Main wing parts.

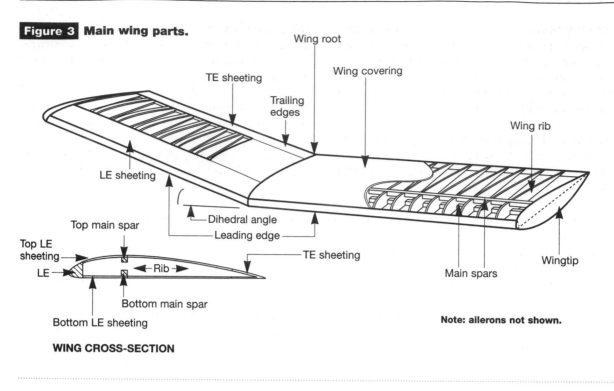

WING CROSS-SECTION

Note: ailerons not shown.

The fuselage includes (see also Figure 2):

• **Firewall**—an upright plywood wall to which the engine or motor is attached; it often supports the nose wheel, too.

• **Formers**—interior wooden pieces mounted at intervals across the inside of the fuselage; they support the sides and give the fuse strength and rigidity.

• **Doublers**—extra layers of balsa or lite-ply that are attached inside the vertical fuselage sides to strengthen specific areas.

• **Stringers, or "longerons"**—long, stick-like parts that support the fabric-covered areas of the fuselage walls and contribute to the model's attractive look.

• **Wing saddle**—the part of the fuselage on which the wing rests and "form fits" into. When the wing is removed, the wing saddle is typically the main opening in the fuselage that allows access to the radio equipment.

■ **WING.** The wing produces lift and its parts include (see Figure 3):

• **Leading edge (LE)**—the wing's front edge; it's rounded to allow the air to flow easily over the wing's top and bottom surfaces.

• **Trailing edge (TE)**—the most aft part of the wing; in cross-section, it has a tapered (wedge) shape and a much sharper edge than the LE to allow the airstreams that pass over and under the wing to come back together easily with minimum drag and turbulence.

• **Ailerons**—the control surfaces that cause the model to roll (see Figures 1 and 4).

• **Wing ribs**—support the upper and lower wing surfaces and so give the wing its "airfoil"-shaped cross-section. As the plane moves through the air, this airfoil shape causes the air to flow over and under the wing in a way that generates the lifting force that allows airplanes to fly.

• **Wingtips**—the very ends of the wing panels, they come in a variety of shapes. Though mostly cosmetic, some wingtip shapes do reduce wingtip drag.

• **Wing root**—the part of the wing that's joined to the fuselage.

• **Main spars**—run lengthwise from wing root to wingtip, giving the wing its longitudinal strength. The main spar can be a single piece of solid wood that passes through the middle of the ribs, or it can be made of two parallel spars attached to the top and bottom of the ribs.

Most of the smaller trainers have only one main spar, but some larger designs have a main spar and an aft spar that is sometimes referred to as a "secondary spar." Double-spar designs may have small sheets of balsa—"shear webs"—connecting the two spars for increased strength.

• **Dihedral**—the upsweep angle of the two wing panels (each half of a wing can be referred to as a panel) relative to the fuselage (see Figure 3). Dihedral helps an airplane roll in response to rudder (yaw) inputs and contributes to its roll stability. The greater the wing's dihedral angle, the more stable the model (to a point).

A thick, angled, plywood part known as a "dihedral brace" is often used to strengthen the wing where the two wing halves join at the wing root. The respective spars of the two wing halves may be glued to the dihedral brace to form a single wing structure.

■ **TAIL FEATHERS**. An airplane's tail has four main parts:
—*horizontal stabilizer*: the small, horizontal tail wing;
—*elevator(s)*: the control surfaces attached to the aft edge of the horizontal stabilizer;
—*vertical fin*: the upright fin structure;
—*rudder*: the control surface attached to the vertical fin.

In most R/C trainers, these parts are made of solid sheet balsa, and the control surfaces such as the rudder and elevators are hinged to the fin and stabilizer. To summarize: the vertical fin supports the rudder, and the horizontal stab supports the elevator(s). The rudder, elevator and (if used) the ailerons (attached to TE of the wing) are the primary control surfaces.

■ **CONTROL SURFACES**. Just like full-size airplanes, our models rely on movable control surfaces to fly and maneuver. For now, we'll concern ourselves with the three basics—elevators, ailerons and rudder—but an airplane might also have flaps, spoilers, leading-edge wing slats and dive brakes.

• **Elevators**—the most often misunderstood by beginners, who often assume that the elevator makes a model go up and come down. This is only partially true. In actuality, the elevators control the plane's attitude (see Figure 4) in the pitch (nose up or down) axis of our model. If the nose pitches up, the angle of the wing relative to the aircraft's forward direction—or to the wind rushing at the airplane—is increased. Whether slight or steep, this wing angle relative to the oncoming air is known as the "angle of attack."

A positive change in pitch, i.e., pointing the nose slightly upward, without an increase in power may not result in a climb. An appropriate angle of attack combined with thrust makes an aircraft climb, i.e, an increase in engine/motor power and, therefore, thrust (which generates airspeed and additional lift, whether at a low or a high angle of attack) increases the rate of climb.

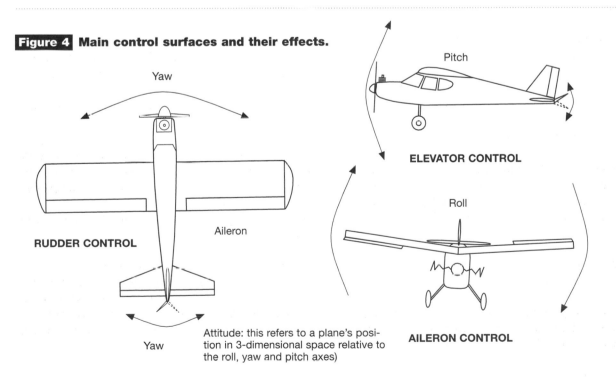

Figure 4 **Main control surfaces and their effects.**

Yaw

Pitch

RUDDER CONTROL

Aileron

ELEVATOR CONTROL

Yaw

Roll

Attitude: this refers to a plane's position in 3-dimensional space relative to the roll, yaw and pitch axes)

AILERON CONTROL

Figure 5 Aerodynamic force of lift.

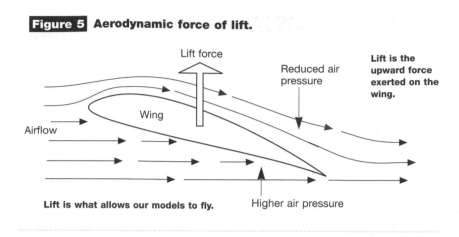

Lift force

Reduced air pressure

Lift is the upward force exerted on the wing.

Wing

Airflow

Lift is what allows our models to fly.

Higher air pressure

• **Ailerons**—on the TE of the main wings, these control surfaces are used to roll a model left or right about its longitudinal axis. Ailerons work opposite to each other so that, for example, when lift is increased on the right wing, it is decreased on the left wing. This difference in lift rolls the model toward the side that has less lift.

• **Rudder**. Rudder input controls the model's attitude with respect to its yaw axis (nose-left or -right movement). In flight, deflecting the rudder swings the nose left or right, and rudder is also important when taxiing on the ground. Rudder is also used with aileron to correct an effect known as "adverse yaw" (for a definition of this, see Appendix 1, "Glossary").

3-CHANNEL, DIHEDRAL SHIPS

When I mentioned ailerons for the first time, I also said "if used." How does a model fly without ailerons? Well, most models with 3-channel radio control (throttle, elevator and rudder), have a fair amount of dihedral (see Figure 3) and, thus, a great degree of built-in stability. When you move the stick to the right for a right turn, the rudder swings to the right and yaws the model's nose to the right.

As the model yaws, the wing (for that matter, the entire plane) essentially pivots relative to the oncoming wind, and the model begins to roll. Although you don't need to understand how it

Figure 6 Basic aerodynamic forces.

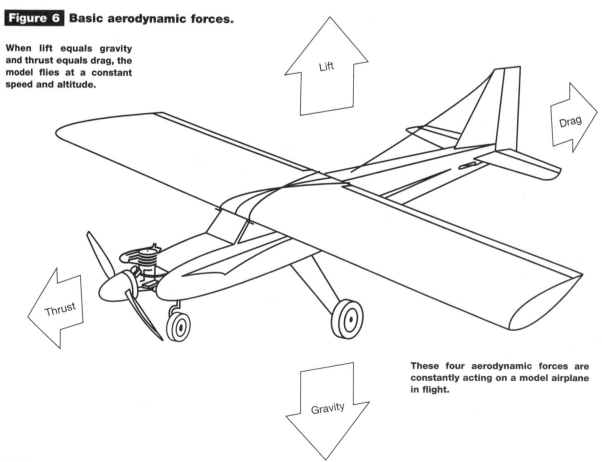

When lift equals gravity and thrust equals drag, the model flies at a constant speed and altitude.

Lift

Drag

Thrust

Gravity

These four aerodynamic forces are constantly acting on a model airplane in flight.

works to see that a right rudder input will result in the model's rolling to the right, here's the briefest of summaries of how it works: the dihedral configuration of the wing, when yawed to the right, exposes more of the underside of the left wing to the oncoming wind and more of the top of the right wing. This effectively raises the left wing's angle of attack and lowers that of the right. This increases the lift generated by the left wing and decreases right-wing lift, all of which also causes the plane to roll to the right.

BASIC AERODYNAMICS

To fully understand how to fly a model airplane, you should know the basics of aerodynamics. Aerodynamic forces—*lift, drag, gravity* and *thrust*—act on models and full-size aircraft in exactly the same manner (see Figure 6).

■ **LIFT**—the upward force generated by the wings while the model is moving forward; it's the force that holds the airplane in the air, and it's the result of the air's flowing over the wing's curved upper and lower surfaces (airfoil).

■ **DRAG**—created by the friction of the airplane against the air as it moves forward. Drag reduces an airplane's speed. Factors that contribute to overall drag are: surface drag, control-surface deflections, flaps and anything else that protrudes from the airplane—landing gear, struts, windshields, etc. The sum of the drag caused by all these is referred to as "parasite drag."

■ **GRAVITY (G force)**—the force that pulls down on the model; it's measured in "G" forces. An airplane in straight and level flight, i.e., not climbing or diving, is subject to 1G. If the model weighs 4 pounds on the ground standing still, it weighs 4 pounds in a 1G situation in flight. In addition to the earth's gravitational pull, centrifugal force can affect the G force encountered by a model. Attach a ball to a length of string and swing it around above your head, and you'll feel the centrifugal force pulling the ball outward from you. When we ask a model to climb, turn or pull out of a dive, centrifugal force effectively adds to its G force, or "weight."

■ **THRUST**—pulls or pushes our model forward. It's created by the propeller as the powerplant spins the prop. Look at a propeller and you'll see that, like a wing, it has an airfoil shape; so in a way, thrust is a forward-pointing lifting force.

Figure 7 More lift than gravity.

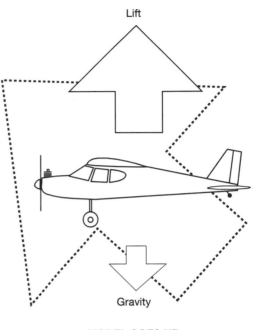

Lift

Gravity

MODEL GOES UP

Figure 8 More gravity than lift.

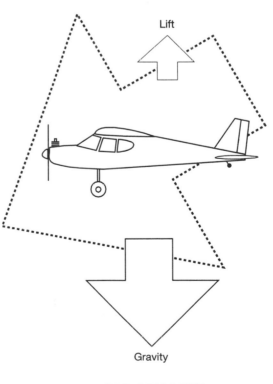

Lift

Gravity

MODEL GOES DOWN

Figure 9 More thrust than drag.

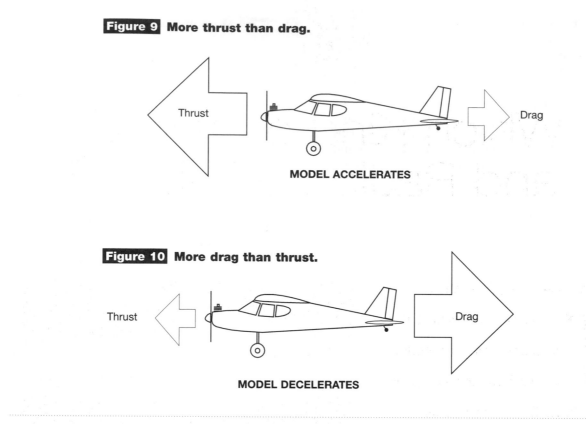

MODEL ACCELERATES

Figure 10 More drag than thrust.

MODEL DECELERATES

As Figure 6 shows, the four forces of aerodynamics are in balance. Lift is countered by gravity and thrust is countered by drag. When you fly your model straight and level at a constant forward speed, the forces are in balance. If thrust is increased, forward speed will increase. If drag is increased, the model will slow down and eventually sink. An increase in lift will make the plane climb, and when gravity overpowers lift, the plans sinks.

In practice, you change the throttle setting and the control-surface deflections to keep your model airborne and flying where you want it to fly. It's a lot easier than all this theory might suggest. The real learning—and the fun—takes place at the flying field with your model and your instructor.

But first, let's take a look at what you need to get into the hobby.

2

Which Kind of Airplane and Radio do I Need?

Which type of airplane should I build?

This is probably what beginners ask most frequently. The answer? Whichever strikes your fancy BUT ... make sure that your first model is a good, strong, stable trainer. Don't try to start with a seductive-looking P-51 Mustang or a multi-engine B-25 bomber; you'll have your hands full just learning the basics. You'll need a forgiving model that, when airborne, allows you lots of

"thinking time" before you have to act. Trust me on this one; many would-be modelers have fallen short of success because they chose the wrong first airplane. A strong construction and stability of design are the keys.

Global's Right Flyer 40 is another good first choice. Note the flat-bottom airfoil that's so typical of trainers.

TYPES OF AIRPLANE

In the early days of the hobby, there was only one type of model airplane to build—all wood; now we're offered a large variety of well-designed kits. Materials such as plastic, fiberglass and foam may be used in place of traditional materials such as balsa, spruce and plywood. Each type has its particular strengths and weaknesses, and which you choose to build is entirely up to you, but you should take your modeling skills (or lack thereof!) into account before purchasing any model. An old saying goes, "To be a winner, do as the winners do." Ask local fliers which models they started with, and benefit from their experience. Here are some of your choices.

■ **ALMOST READY TO FLY (ARF).** ARF kits supply models that leave very little work for you to do. Some are assembled at the factory and come to you built. Sub-assemblies can be built and installed in anywhere from 10 to 20 hours. The fuselage, tail components and wing halves are complete (often finished with covering film, too), and the kits include landing gear and basic hardware such as wheels, fuel tank, engine/motor mount, pushrods,

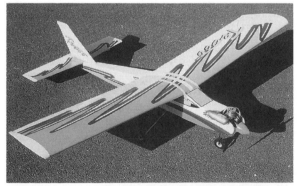

This joint effort by Thunder Tiger and Horizon Hobby—the T-2000 ARF—was designed to make learning to fly easy and fun. Instead of written instructions, it comes with videotape that guides you through its construction.

nuts, screws, bolts and washers.

ARFs are available in all wood (already covered), foam and fiberglass (already painted) and a construction involving a laminated foam skin over a wooden structure—among other configurations.

ARF kits rarely include full-size plans because there is no real building; they do include an instruction booklet and perhaps some decals.

But before you break out the glue, first sit down and read the instructions carefully. Though ARFs are relatively easy to build, they require that you follow the

The Hangar 9 Cessna, available from Horizon Hobby Distributors is a good ARF trainer. It has attractive lines and wheel pants and comes with an attractive printed covering already applied.

The Easy Fly 40 from Horizon Hobby Distributors is typical of wooden ARFs in that it has a strong, box-construction fuselage, long tail and nose moments (for pitch stability) and a wing that comes in two pieces that must be epoxied together.

set assembly order and the procedures given in the instructions. Follow the instructions carefully, and you will maximize your chances of success.

■ **ALMOST READY TO COVER (ARC).** These models come "framed," i.e., most of the wooden parts have been glued and assembled, so "final assembly" goes quite quickly. They basically require as much assembling as ARFs, but many modelers think that ARCs have an added appeal in that they allow you to cover and finish the aircraft according to your own preferences. Instead of having a Super Wizbang trainer that looks exactly like the next

Super Wizbang trainer, your model can be of any color and have any type of graphics; it can be unique. Some ARCs have foam-core wings, but the big difference between ARFs and ARCs is that you will have to cover a framed-up model.

ARCs also require that you have a few more tools for sanding the wood and for cutting and applying the covering and heat-shrinking it to the frame. You'll decide which type of covering material to use (see Chapter 8).

Altech Marketing's ARF Tame Cat is a good first model disguised as a sport-scale fighter. It's also available as an ARC.

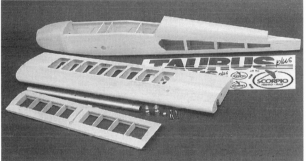

Though it isn't a basic trainer, the Taurus Plus is a good example of an ARC model. It comes completely built, but the wings have to be glued together and the tail must be joined to the fuselage; then you can cover it in any way you like.

a relatively simple task; you might even be ready for the flying field on the same day as you buy the kit (well, if you're a methodical builder and this is your very first model, maybe the day *after* that). Rarely are painting and finishing required; just stick the decals on. These models tend to be smaller, but nothing beats their simplicity and speed of construction.

■ **DURA PLANE.** The Dura Trainer and Dura Bat models offered by Great Planes are also good choices for your first R/C airplane. Very little gluing is involved because most of the parts are bolted together or joined with rubber bands. Aluminum, rigid formed plastic, balsa and foam (the wing) are the main materials used. Leave the foam wing uncovered, or apply a low-temperature, iron-on film such as Oracover. The fuselage is a combination of a square plastic tube (household downspout material) and an extruded-aluminum tail boom—not too attractive, but very rugged.

■ **FOAM AND PLASTIC.** Foam and plastic trainers sometimes come in a package deal that includes a radio and an engine or motor, and many are suitable for beginners. Assembling this type of model is

Cox offers several "foamie" trainers, including the R/C Skybird and the R/C Commander. These foam and plastic models use ½A Cox engines for power, and their long, polyhedral wings give them excellent roll stability.

A first trainer typically has a relatively short life, and one could argue that as long as it flies well, it doesn't matter what a first model looks like. When the "Dura" models were introduced, they were advertised as being "crashproof," and for the most part, this claim is true; I have had Dura Plane mod-

You could learn to fly with a glider. This is Thunder Tiger's Windstar ARF.

els hit the ground really hard and suffer only a broken prop and a loose wing (attached with rubber bands). The model was usually back in the air in a few minutes—no worse for wear.

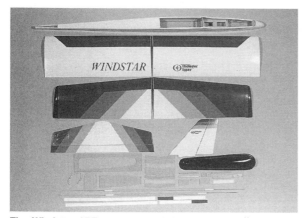

The Windstar ARF comes out of the box like this—no construction required; simply join the prebuilt parts and install a 2-channel radio.

■ **CORRUGATED PLASTIC.** Built using the fold-and-glue method, these quite different-looking, highly durable models have some very interesting features. There's no finishing because the plastic is colored, and they're easy to build with contact cement. There are many choices of corrugated-plastic models, and their construction takes considerably less time than it does with most of the other types of model.

■ **BUILT-UP WOOD.** Open an all-wood kit, and you know right away that it's a different ballgame from the one you play with ARFs and ARCs. These classic models are made of traditional balsa, spruce and lite-ply, and they were predominant during the early years of our hobby. Wooden kits are still the most plentiful on the hobby-shop shelves (although ARFs are of growing popularity), and there is a truly wonderful selection.

If you enjoy building and tinkering and enjoy working with wood—often already cut into the appropriate parts—you won't begrudge spending time on making your first aircraft. The wood may be die-cut or, in the newer kits, laser-cut (laser cutting is very precise). The kit will also include numerous, long, balsa sticks, small balsa blocks, hardware and a full set of plans.

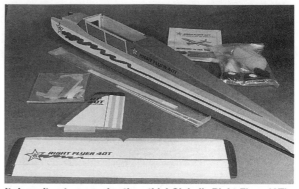

It doesn't get any easier than this! Global's Right Flyer 40T's fuselage is a box structure to which you glue the tail and then add hardware. Engine and radio installation are covered in the instruction manual.

If you choose to build a wooden kit, be prepared for the construction work that lies ahead. All-wood kits often cost less than foam and plastic ones; some of the imported, wood ARFs also cost slightly less than the total cost of a raw kit and the needed accessories and supplies!

Building a wooden kit offers the advantage that when it's finished, you will know exactly how it was put together. When you need to repair it (and you will), you'll be better prepared for the task. Building it will also give you a much greater feeling of accomplishment; for many, building is a very big part of the hobby—one with its own set of goals and rewards.

It's important that you learn to read plans and follow the instructions; and you'll also need basic building skills such as cutting, gluing, clamping and sanding. But there really isn't anything diffi-

With its big, high-lift wing and strong fuselage, the all-wood Flying King from BTE can be built in several configurations; here, it's a tail-dragger with flaps.

Almost crash-proof, the Dura Plane series of airplanes make good trainers. The Aerobat .40 shown here has ailerons.

This U.S. AirCore corrugated-plastic model uses the fold-and-glue construction method.

The Dura Plane trainer may not be beautiful, but it is sturdy and easy to build; in a trainer, looks aren't everything.

The Sig Mfg. Kadet is typical of built-up wooden models. It's very light and strong, and thousands of modelers have learned to fly with this series.

cult or mysterious about any of this. Again, if you follow the manufacturer's instructions, you'll be well on your way to completing your first R/C model.

RADIO SYSTEMS

In addition to a good reliable trainer aircraft, you also need a radio system—a transmitter and a receiver—to control your airplane. It's a pilot's link to his airplane, and a typical radio will control it farther than you can see; you can be confident about controlling the actions of the control surfaces even when you can't actually see them. In a full-size aircraft, the pilot sees and feels everything that the airplane is doing, but the R/C pilot must learn to judge his airplane's actions from a distance.

Develop your depth perception through practice, and learn to anticipate the aircraft's movement through the air—a skill that can be developed through flight training (see Chapter 10).

A basic radio package consists of a 3- or 4-channel transmitter (TX), a receiver (RX), three or more servos (the "muscles" that move the control rods that move the control surfaces), a battery pack that powers the RX and a switch harness that turns it on and off. There's usually a battery charging jack wired into the switch harness.

The radio system also comes with instructions, a charger, servo-mounting hardware and a red flag and set of radio-frequency (RF) numbers that have to be attached to your TX antenna. These numbers identify your radio's transmitting frequency—very important when you're at the flying field.

Radios are available with FM (frequency modulation), AM (amplitude modulation) and PCM (pulse-code modulation) systems. AM systems are the least expensive, but all will control your trainer equally well. Talk to your hobby shop about the bells and whistles offered by the other systems (details of which are beyond the scope of this book). All modern R/C radios have plug-and-socket connectors to complete the wiring connections—no soldering required. Some brands have their own unique wire-plug connector, and some have connectors that are compatible with several brands of radio. All operate on the same electronic principles.

The major aircraft radio brands include Airtronics,

The Wingo ARF distributed by Hobby Lobby is a Speed 400-powered foam and wood model; extremely easy to assemble and fly.

The Hitec Focus 4 is a good 4-channel radio: its TX has two control sticks, trim levers, a collapsible antenna and an RF meter to check signal strength.

If you think you'll be in the hobby for the long haul, a 6-channel radio such as the XP642 from JR would be a wise investment. When you've mastered the basics, you'll already have an advanced radio for sport flying.

Futaba, Hitec RCD and JR, to name only a few.

■ TRANSMITTER (TX)—the "box" you hold in your hands and from which you operate (control) your model. It has a long antenna, one or two control sticks, trim levers, an on/off switch and a battery-charging jack. Most transmitters have a radio-frequency (RF) meter that indicates voltage and thereby tells the strength of the transmitter's signal. The RF meter's face usually has green and red areas in its display; when the needle enters the red area, it's time to stop flying and charge the batteries.

The most popular type of transmitter has two main control sticks that allow you to control the four basic functions. Typically:

A typical flight pack consists of a receiver (RX), a Ni-Cd battery pack and three or four servos. Not shown is the wire harness with on/off switch and charging jack.

• Left stick controls:
—*throttle*: push it forward to increase throttle; pull it back to decrease throttle;
—*rudder*: move it to the left and to right.

• Right stick controls:
—*elevator*: move it forward and backward;
—*ailerons*: move it left and right.

Radios with more than four channels can control additional functions:
—*retractable landing gear;*
—*flaps;*
—*spoilers;*
—*bomb drops;*
—*lighting systems.*
In this book, however, we'll concern ourselves with the four basic controls.

If you fly a 3-channel, dihedral airplane (no ailerons and main wings are angled up slightly), roll control will be operated by activating the rudder servos with the right TX stick, i.e., in place of aileron control.

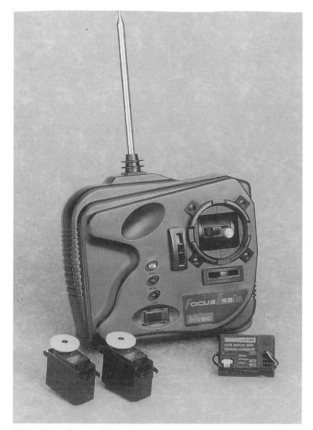

This Hitec Focus II system is typical of those included in package deals (the radio and model come in one box). The small lights indicate RF strength.

■ **RECEIVER (RX)**—the part of the radio system that receives the TX signal and converts it into electrical impulses that control the system's "muscles"—the servos. A long, thin wire—the antenna—comes out of it. Never cut this wire or coil it, or you'll greatly reduce your radio's operating range, and that might cause you to lose control of the model shortly after takeoff.

Both the RX and TX have crystals that determine the radio's frequency, or channel. You can buy extra receivers and servos so you'll be able to operate two or more model airplanes without having to buy another complete radio system. The more sophisticated radios can "remember" the settings for several models, so if you use your radio for more than one model, you can flip to the appropriate setting for each one.

■ **SERVOS**—the radio system's "workers"; they are used to move the control surfaces. Each consists of a small motor, a gear train, an electronic control circuit and a feedback potentiometer (pot). The

servo has an output arm, or wheel, that is connected to a pushrod inside the model. When the servo moves, it pushes or pulls the pushrod, which, in turn, moves the control surface.

The TX is always sending a signal. When you move a control stick, the signal is changed slightly, and the RX picks up this change. The RX then decodes the signal and sends it to a specific servo. The result is "proportional" control: move the stick a little, and the control surface moves a little; move the stick a lot, and the control surface moves accordingly.

■ **BATTERIES**. R/C systems typically use nickel-cadmium (Ni-Cd) battery cells to power the TX and the RX. The TX typically requires a 9.6-volt (9.6V) battery, and the RX usually operates on 4.8 volts. Each Ni-Cd cell is rated at 1.2 volts, and the cells are wired together to make battery packs. Typically, the RX for a trainer requires a 450- to 600-milliamp-hour (mAh) pack while the

Servos come in many sizes—from micro to giant scale—and they're the workers in our radio systems.

TX requires an 800- to 1000mAh pack. They will come with your radio system.

Giant-scale models and models that have many servos require packs with larger capacities: 1000mAh and even 1500mAh. For your trainer and for general sport-flying models, a 450 to 650mAh pack will be just fine.

The chargers that are included with most radio systems will charge the RX and TX batteries at the same time. Simply plug the charger into the wall and then connect the leads to the TX and RX. On the day or evening before you plan to fly, charge your radio system for between 15 and 24 hours for a full charge. After that, you can expect the system to operate safely for about 2 hours of flying time before you'll need a new receiver-pack charge.

Ni-Cd battery packs: the one on the left powers the RX flight pack and the 9.6V pack on the right powers the TX.

You don't need a radio system for every model you own. Servos, switches and receivers are available separately, so you can have several flight packs that work with one transmitter.

Considering that an average flight lasts between 10 and 15 minutes and that you'll probably fly three or four flights on a typical flying day, that's a large safety margin. You'll be checking battery-power levels along the way in any case.

Under that little cover is the crystal that determines which frequency your system transmits on.

As with model airplane kits, radios come with instructions, and they're the first thing to look at before you turn on your new radio. With proper care and charging, your radio system should last for many years.

In the next chapter, we'll look at the R/C model's powerplant.

The Power Source

Model airplanes can be powered in a variety of ways: by 2-stroke or 4-stroke engines or electric motors. There are benefits and drawbacks to each, and the choice is up to you. We will concern ourselves with glow-powered engines and electric motors.

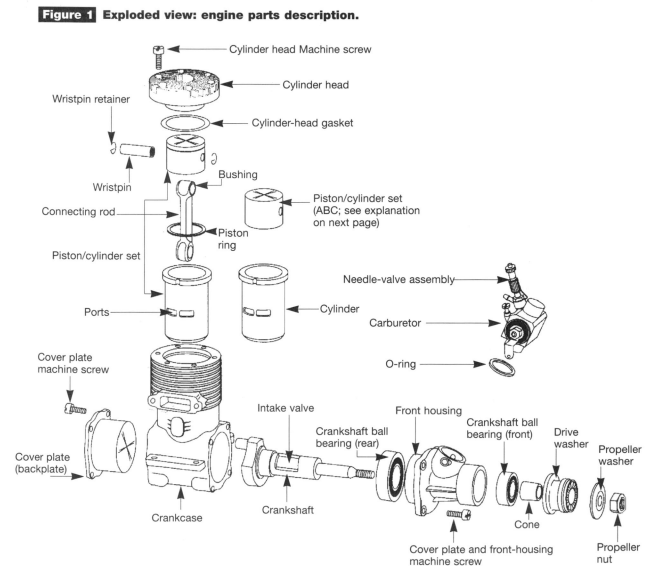

If an airplane is to fly, it must have something in the nose to pull it—this O.S. 32 engine, for example. R/C engines are not difficult to operate, but careful treatment and a proper regard for safety are vital.

TWO-STROKE ENGINES

These are the most popular types. They have a good power-to-weight ratio (you get a lot of power for each ounce of weight) and few moving parts, and they're relatively inexpensive. Maintenance is very easy, and with proper break-in, a 2-stroke engine will last many years.

In size, these engines range from .010 cubic inch (ci) to over 3ci, but .40 to .60ci are the most used sizes. Also very popular are .049 (½A), .10, .15, .25, .32, .45, .46, .50 and .90ci.

All model airplanes have a recommended engine-size range, but most perform best when powered by an engine that's toward the top of the range. There's nothing worse than having an under-powered model, especially when you are trying to learn how to fly.

Figure 1 **Exploded view: engine parts description.**

Cylinder head Machine screw
Cylinder head
Wristpin retainer
Cylinder-head gasket
Bushing
Wristpin
Piston/cylinder set (ABC; see explanation on next page)
Connecting rod
Piston ring
Piston/cylinder set
Needle-valve assembly
Cylinder
Ports
Carburetor
Cover plate machine screw
O-ring
Intake valve
Front housing
Crankshaft ball bearing (front)
Cover plate (backplate)
Crankshaft ball bearing (rear)
Drive washer
Propeller washer
Crankcase
Crankshaft
Cone
Cover plate and front-housing machine screw
Propeller nut

ILLUSTRATION BY CHRISTOPHER MENDOLA

Figure 2 Two-stroke engine operation.

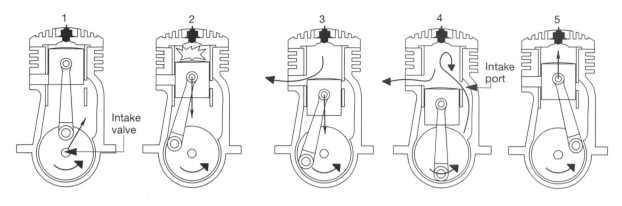

1. As the piston reaches top dead center, a new charge of fuel/air mixture is drawn into the crankcase because of the low pressure created by the piston's upward motion.

2. The current fuel/air mixture is then compressed by the piston in the combustion chamber, and it heats up and is ignited by the glow plug. This forces the piston downward.

3. As the piston comes down, it opens the exhaust port, and the spent fuel charge begins to exit the combustion chamber.

At the same time, the piston compresses the new fuel/air mixture charge in the crankcase.

4. At bottom dead center, the piston opens the bypass port and the new fuel-mixture charge flows from the crankcase into the combustion chamber as the last of the spent charge leaves.

5. The piston comes back up and seals the exhaust and bypass port, and the entire sequence of events begins again.

ENGINE TERMINOLOGY

You should know a few basic engine terms (see Figure 1):
• **ABC**—refers to the materials used to make the engine: aluminum (A) piston, fitted inside a brass (B) sleeve that's chrome-plated (C).
• **Case**—the main body of the engine.
• **Connecting rod (conrod)**—the part that attaches the piston to the crankshaft. The conrod has a bushing at either end and is connected to the piston with a wristpin and to the crankcase with the crankpin.
• **Cylinder head**—the part on top of the engine; it's usually bolted into place with four to six bolts. In its center is a threaded hole for the glow plug.
• **Ports**—channels, or openings, inside the engine case that transfer the fuel and air mixture from the crankcase to the combustion chamber. The ports are opened and closed by the upward and downward motion of the piston.
• **Sleeve**—the cylinder lining; it houses and guides the piston; it is separate from the engine case and has openings (ports) cut in its side.

See Figure 1 to identify these and other key engine components.

ENGINE BREAKDOWN

The engine case usually has three parts:
• **front housing**—the case that surrounds the crankshaft;

• **crankcase**—the main case on which the cylinder head sits;
• **backplate**—the plate that seals the back of the engine.

Some engines have a two-piece case, but the "internals" of all engines are the same.

The crankshaft is supported within the front housing by ball bearings or bushings and has a threaded front end. Bushings, like bearings, are machine parts in which other parts turn; bushings are often used on less expensive engines (see bearings in Figure 1). A prop nut and a prop washer hold the prop securely against the thrust washer at the front of the engine. At its rear, the crankshaft has a counterweight and a crankpin that engages the bottom end of the connecting rod.

The connecting rod is attached to the piston with a wristpin. The piston fits inside the engine's sleeve, which itself fits into and is supported by the engine case. The head sits atop the cylinder and its inner sleeve, and the space between the top of the piston and the bottom of the head is the combustion chamber.

BASIC 2-STROKE ENGINE OPERATION

A 2-stroke engine makes one revolution for every power cycle (see Figure 2). As the piston moves upward in the cylinder, it compresses a fresh charge of fuel. The fuel/air mixture heats up and is ignited by the glow plug. The piston's upward motion cre-

One of the most popular 2-stroke engines of all time has to be the Cox ½A (.049ci). Here, a Cox Tee Dee .049 is shown mounted on a combination fuel tank and engine mount. It turns a 6x3 prop.

ates a negative pressure inside the crankcase below the piston, and this draws air and fuel in from the carb through the intake valve.

The combustion of the fuel/air mixture forces the piston downward in the cylinder, which now compresses the fresh charge of fuel. As the piston travels down and the hollow crankshaft rotates, the intake valve is closed, and the intake ports are opened. The compressed fuel charge passes upward through the ports and is directed into the combustion chamber (see Figure 2). This happens just as the spent fuel charge is exiting the combustion chamber through the exhaust port. As the piston moves upward again, it closes the exhaust port, opens the intake valve below, and the entire process is then repeated.

FOUR-STROKE ENGINES

Four-stroke engines are popular because they have a wide power band (they provide great torque at lower rpm) and sound so nice while they're running. They are, however, more expensive and more complicated than 2-strokes and require more maintenance if they're to operate properly.

Instead of having intake and exhaust ports, a 4-stroke engine has intake and exhaust valves just like the family car's engine does (see Figure 3). A cam assembly is driven by the crankshaft, and there are lifter rods, tappets and valve springs. When adjusted properly, 4-strokes produce a fair amount of power, but they're at their peak at a lower rpm range than 2-stroke engines of the same size. In comparison, the power of a .90 4-stroke is roughly equivalent to that of a .60 2-stroke engine.

Saito offers a large selection of 4-stroke engines, which develop their power at a lower and wider power band and sound great when running properly. Note the rod tubes at the front of the engine.

Figure 3 Four-stroke engine operation.

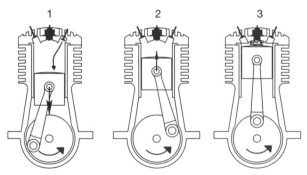
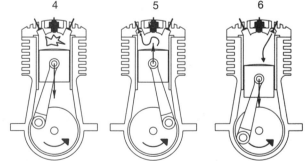

1. Intake: the piston comes down, the intake valve opens, and the fuel charge is drawn into the combustion chamber.

2. Compression: the piston comes up as the intake valve closes and compresses the fuel charge.

3. Ignition: when the piston is at top dead center, the glow plug ignites the compressed fuel charge.

4. The fuel mixture rapidly expands and forces the piston downward.

5. Exhaust: the piston comes back up again while the exhaust valve opens and the spent fuel charge is expelled.

6. The piston goes back down, and the entire sequence of events begins again.

START-UP AND BREAK-IN

A just-out-of-the-box, brand-new engine needs special handling before it can be run at full throttle. Don't just bolt an engine to your model and go to the flying field. Some modelers say it's OK to do this, but the first time out, you should play it safe and do a proper engine break-in at home where you have all your tools and supplies. Short, well-lubricated runs break an engine in gently because they allow the parts to seat and fit together gradually.

When you break in an engine, you are trying to gradually wear all the parts so they match one another precisely. To operate properly, all engines must be broken in—some take longer than others. If you run an engine without first breaking it in, it will run very hot because of excess friction, and the odds are that localized heat will damage it. Basically, we're most concerned about the piston/sleeve fit.

First, install a new glow plug—*properly*! Gently tighten the glow plug down just snugly; don't tighten it with a lot of force, or you may inadvertently strip the aluminum threads in the engine head. Fill the fuel tank with a 2-stroke fuel that contains 5 to 10 percent nitromethane and 18 to 20 percent oil. Attach the fuel line to the needle-valve assembly (see Figure 4); make sure that the

Figure 4 Carburetor breakdown.

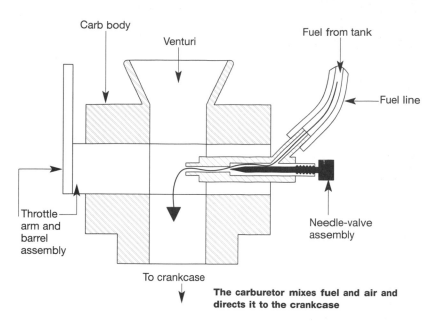

The carburetor mixes fuel and air and directs it to the crankcase

line is not kinked and doesn't rest against the engine case, which will get hot as the engine runs. Attach a propeller of the recommended size, and install the prop washer and prop nut. Snug the nut down and then tighten it somewhat firmly, but with a short wrench, e.g., 6 inches.

Open the engine's needle valve at least 4 full turns, and open the throttle fully. Put your thumb over the air-intake venturi (see Figure 4), and flip the prop counterclockwise several times. You will see fuel start to flow through the fuel line and into the carb. Once the fuel has reached the carb, close the throttle to about ¼, and hook up your glow-plug battery. Flip the prop over with a chicken stick (a purpose-built tool for turning props by hand) or an electric torque starter until the engine catches and starts to run. When the engine has warmed up a little, open the throttle all the way, and let the engine run for about 10 minutes at a very rich, low power setting (see Figure 5). Then stop the engine and let it cool off. Repeat the process several times, and gradually lean out the engine by turning the needle valve clockwise a

Figure 5 Throttle barrel.

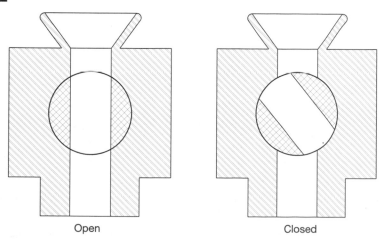

The throttle barrel controls how much air/fuel mixture enters the carb. When the throttle is open, the engine gets more fuel/air, and it runs at high rpm. When the barrel is closed, less of the mixture enters the engine and it runs more slowly.

couple of clicks each time. Don't let the engine run at high rpm, i.e., at a lean setting, until you have run at least five or six tanks of fuel through it with the engine running rich.

You will know that your engine has been properly broken in when it runs consistently without overheating and has a very good transition from idle to full throttle. And remember: it is always better to operate your engine a few clicks on the rich side because this helps cool the engine by virtue of fuel flow and decreases rpm.

Proper break-in is very important to the well-being of your expensive engine. Follow its manufacturer's suggested break-in procedure, and always use filtered fuel.

• **Low-end setting.** Before you fly your model, it must have a very reliable idle. Some engines have a single needle valve and a small bleed hole that is used for the low-end, or idle, fuel/air mixture setting; others have two needles—a large (main) needle for the high-end setting and a smaller one for idle. When you break in your engine, you will also learn to adjust the low-end mixture setting. Start with the engine's factory setting; it's usually pretty close to the correct setting.

Model airplane engines use glow plugs to ignite the fuel charge. There are several kinds of plug, so check your engine's instruction manual to find out which type you should use. Note that the glow plug shown above has a bar across its bottom—an idler bar; it shields the element from fresh fuel charge and thus helps the engine to idle reliably.

If you bring an engine to idle and it dies, the low-end fuel/air mixture setting is too lean. You must increase the amount of fuel drawn into the carb at idle. If the engine settles into an idle but then burbles or dies when the throttle is opened again, the low-end mixture setting is too rich, and you must decrease the amount of fuel entering the carb at idle. It's a balance.

An opening In the bottom of the glow plug contains a platinum coil. This is the element, and it glows red hot when energized by a starter battery.

With the twin-needle-valve carb design, you use the idle needle valve to adjust how much fuel enters the carb. In the air-bleed design, you use the air-bleed screw to adjust how much air enters the carb during idle. The first design adjusts the fuel; the second adjusts the air, but both achieve the same result: air/fuel mixture adjustment. Both types of carb work well, but the more powerful engines usually rely on the twin-needle valve carb.

CARE AND MAINTENANCE
If you care for your engine properly from the start, you will get maximum power and longevity from it. This care should start on the day you take it home. Most engines come with Allen wrenches to loosen and tighten the screws; keep these in a safe place, and if you do lose one, replace it with one of the same size.

An engine-maintenance check often begins with the removal of the engine's backplate and a check inside the crankcase for metal shavings and other debris. Also remove the head and check the combustion chamber. Squirt 3-in-1 oil into the engine and turn the engine over. Lubricate the bearings and the conrod bushings (see Figure 1). Check to make sure the ports in the sleeve match the ports that have been cast or machined in the case.

Now reassemble the engine and tighten the screws in a "criss-crossing" pattern. Do not use Loctite or any other thread-locking compound on the case screws or head screws. It is not required and will hamper future maintenance efforts. If you use it, you might end up stripping the threads in the screw holes.

Never force any part that won't go on or move easily. An engine is mostly made of aluminum, and it is very easy to strip the screw-hole threads. To tighten the prop nut, always use a wrench of the proper size; never use vise grips or pliers. A 6-inch adjustable wrench is a handy tool to carry in your field box.

After the day's last flight, drain all the fuel out of the tank, and run the engine dry of fuel. Then squirt in some after-run oil to coat the inside surfaces and prevent them from corroding. Alcohol-based fuels attract moisture, and an unprotected engine will corrode, especially its ball bearings. Oil is inexpensive insurance for long engine life.

ELECTRIC MOTORS

The AstroFlight 15 cobalt motor has to be one of the kings of electric motors. A number of the available—and almost silent—electric powerplants can easily power many of today's popular trainers.

In areas where noise is a concern and for those who like to fly gliders but don't have space for a winch or a high-start launching system, electric motors offer an easy, efficient way to get your model into the air. Scale models can be powered by motors as can "multi-engine" models and ducted-fan models.

You can climb to altitude several times on a single battery charge. With an electric-powered glider, on a single battery charge, flights of 30 minutes are not unusual.

Motors vary in size and the number of battery cells needed to power them. For a detailed analysis of prop selection for your motor, see the directions that come with it (and see Chapter 13, "Prop Talk").

There are two basic types of motor—those with brushes (brushed) and those without (brushless).

• **Brushed motors.** These use brushes to conduct electricity to the commutator, which then conducts the current to the armature, which consists of plates wrapped with wire. The commutator (comm) and armature (arm)—two parts of the same assembly—spin in the middle of the motor because of magnetic fields generated by the current provided by the battery. Magnets bonded to the inside of the motor case interact with these fields, and that makes the comm/armature turn.

• **Brushless motors** have the armature wound on the inside of the bell (the "bell" is the motor case), and a shaft-mounted magnet rotates in the middle. A special speed controller sequentially sends current through the armature to spin the shaft that holds the magnets. There are no brushes and no commutator, so—and this is a benefit—no electrical arcing between the brush and the commutator. Brushless motors run cooler and are slightly more efficient, but they also require special speed controllers and are more expensive.

If you power your model with a motor, you'll need support equipment (see Figure 6). The basic power system consists of the motor, an electronic speed-control unit, an arming switch, a fuse and a battery pack. Most battery packs are made up of Ni-Cd (nickel-

This Astro 805PG brushless motor uses a planetary gearbox. Powered by 7, 2000mAh Ni-Cds, it will spin an 11x8 Cam propeller at 6,5000rpm.

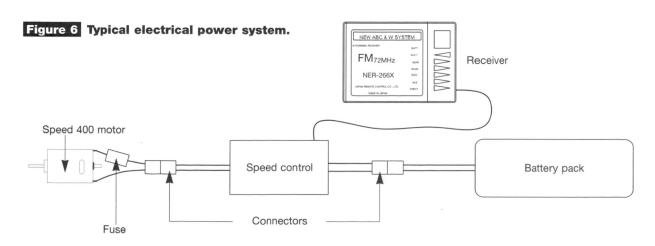

Figure 6 **Typical electrical power system.**

Speed 400 motor

Fuse

Connectors

NEW ABC & W SYSTEM
8-CHANNEL RECEIVER
FM 72MHz
NER-266X
JAPAN REMOTE CONTROL CO., LTD
MADE IN JAPAN

Receiver

Speed control

Battery pack

cadmium) cells that are usually of 1.2V sub-C size. A 6-cell battery pack produces 7.2 volts and a 7-cell pack produces 8.4 volts. Their capacity is rated in milliamp hours (mAh) and, depending on your amp draw, you can expect run times of 3 to 7 minutes from 6- and 7-cell packs (amp draw is directly affected by prop size and pitch). As you gain in skill, you'll learn to extend flight times by gliding and taking advantage of thermals to conserve battery power. Some airplanes, e.g., the Wingo trainer from Hobby Lobby, will fly for 11 minutes on an 8-cell pack. New nickel-metal-hydride batteries—just coming onto the market as this book goes to print—can extend the Wingo's flight times to beyond 15 minutes of continuous power.

Gearboxes such as this one from Master Airscrew can be bought separately and then added to your direct-drive motor.

A motor may have a direct drive or a geared drive. Which you choose should depend on your application: do you want a shorter but high-powered flight (higher rpm) or a longer, more docile performance (lower rpm)? Is your plane "draggy" (geared

A typical motor-mount setup: two metal clamps screwed to hardwood beams securely hold the motor. This is a gearbox-equipped Graupner Speed 500.

preferred) or a "racer" (direct drive)? Either can work perfectly well on a trainer.

• **Direct-drive motors**—good for small, high-speed pylon racers.

• **Geared motors**—best for gliders and scale models.

Another consideration is prop size. The larger the prop, the more likely you'll need a geared motor. It all comes down to matching your motor's power requirements to efficient amp draws. But this can be the subject of a book entirely dedicated to electrics.

SPEED CONTROLLERS

Electronic speed controllers are more efficient than mechanical ones and allow much longer run times for a given battery and motor setup. ESCs are known as "high-frequency" controllers because they use highly efficient electronic switches to control a motor's speed. The switches open and close many thousands of times per second and, in general, are better suited to handling the amps and heat produced in electric-powered models.

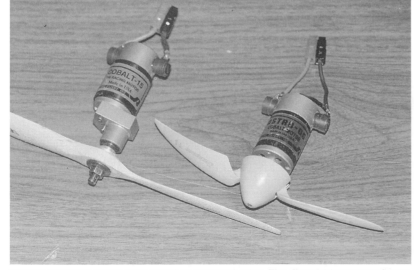

Motors may have direct drive (right) or a geared drive. The direct-drive motor shown turns a Graupner folding prop and spinner.

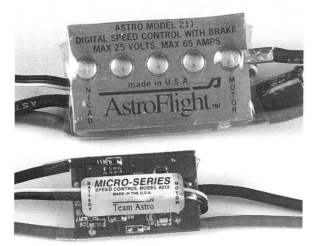

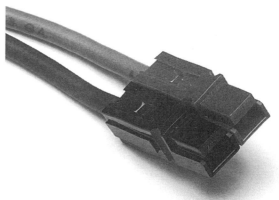

Wire connectors like these from Sermos allow quick battery changes. There are several types of connector.

Electronic speed controllers work extremely well. The AstroFlight 212D (in the back) and the 215 are particularly light and reliable.

For a typical day at the flying field, you'll need:
• a 12V DC field battery charger (usually run off your car's battery);
• two or three 6- or 7-cell battery packs (one in the model, one hooked up to the charger and one ready to go);
• a few extra props—just in case.
After a day's electric flying, there's no clean-up, and many people just like not having to tote a can of fuel, a fuel pump and a muffler to keep the model quiet.

It's really all up to you.

The Power Peak Infinity delta peak charger/cycler made by Robbe is capable of charging from 1 to 30 cells

The Workshop

To build a model airplane, you'll need the proper tools and a place to work—somewhere that makes it easy for you to have fun while you work. Most of modeling's frustrations come not from the tasks required but from not having the correct tools for the job or the right place to do it (see Figure 1, which depicts an ideal workshop layout).

When most people get into the hobby, they already have the basic tools and skills they need, but they might not have a workshop—a place that's theirs alone. Making a small workbench in an unused room, the garage, or the basement is the first thing to do.

WORKBENCH

A workbench can be as simple as a piece of salvaged, construction-site plywood placed across two sawhorses (see Figure 2). It can also be a beautifully hand-crafted, laminated, hardwood countertop with a cabinet base and drawers for all your tools. Somewhere between these two examples, there should be something that matches your style.

Your workbench must be strong and have a perfectly flat, warp-free surface. While living in a small apartment, I once built many models on a 6x3-foot piece of ½-inch-thick plywood that I stored underneath my bed. Now, after 13 years of living in my present home, my workshop occupies about half of my basement.

An inexpensive, hollow-core, interior-grade lauan-wood door from a home-improvement center makes an excellent bench top because it's unlikely to warp. (You can't build straight models on a warped building surface.) Such doors are about 7 feet long and about

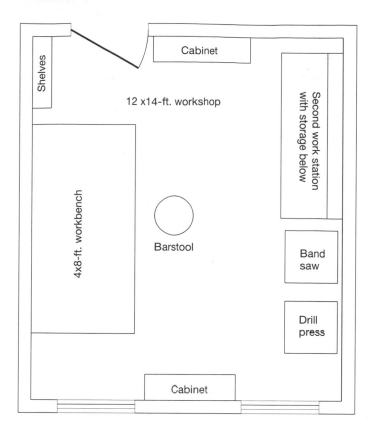

Figure 1 Typical workshop layout.

Shelves

Cabinet

12 x14-ft. workshop

Second work station with storage below

4x8-ft. workbench

Barstool

Band saw

Drill press

Cabinet

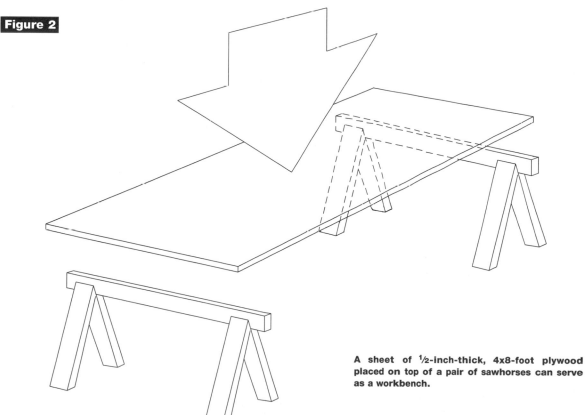

Figure 2

A sheet of ½-inch-thick, 4x8-foot plywood placed on top of a pair of sawhorses can serve as a workbench.

2½ to 3 feet wide. You might even find one in the "dented and scratched" section at a fraction of its original price. Even if one side is marred, the other side might be perfect for your bench top.

As an alternative to sawhorse "legs," you can make a pine-board framework to support your workbench. Make legs out of 1x4-inch pine pieces, adding cross-bracing for support and rigidity (see Figure 3). Between the legs, add a plywood storage shelf.

Just remember to build straight and support your workbench properly to prevent it from warping.

Workbench lighting is also very important; try to have it overhead to eliminate glare and shadows. Two 4-foot-long, fluorescent utility lights hanging about 3 or 4 feet above the bench keep everything well lit and minimize eye strain.

If your workbench is against a wall, mount a pegboard on the wall and hang your most often used supplies and tools there. If you have a place for every tool and keep each where it belongs when you aren't using it, you'll spend less time looking

If you have the space, it's great to have separate work areas for different tasks. This small, but very organized, paint area is dedicated to the messy job of spray painting models. The small opening in the left wall is an exhaust fan.

for them and more time building your model. Organization is an important part of building efficiently and maximizing your model-building enjoyment.

MORE SPACE

A second work table is a plus, especially if you have enough room to put it in the center of your workshop so that you can use it as an assembly station

---

Figure 3 Workbench details.

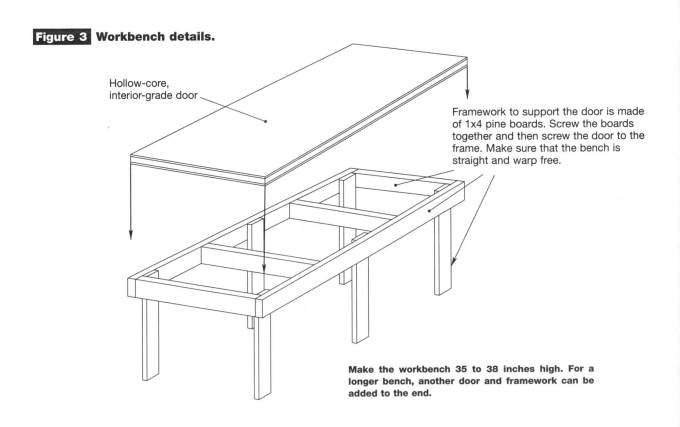

Hollow-core, interior-grade door

Framework to support the door is made of 1x4 pine boards. Screw the boards together and then screw the door to the frame. Make sure that the bench is straight and warp free.

Make the workbench 35 to 38 inches high. For a longer bench, another door and framework can be added to the end.

that you can walk all the way around; you can attach the wings and assemble the tail section directly on the fuselage without banging the fuselage into a wall or a cabinet. Also, having a second place to work allows you to separate tasks and have specific tools at hand just where you need them.

If you have the room, consider separate areas for woodworking, soldering, covering and/or painting and radio installation. Think about your building requirements, and then design a workplace to suit your budget, working style and available space.

BASIC TOOLS

If you attended shop class in school, you have the skills required to build a model airplane. The tools you'll need are not expensive, and most can easily be stored in a single toolbox.

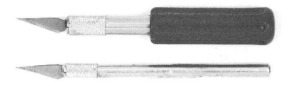

A hobby knife is the most used tool; separate blades are available.

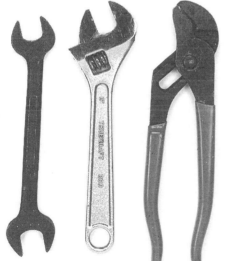

Wrenches of several sizes and styles are needed to tighten and loosen nuts and bolts.

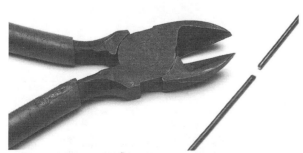

You'll need diagonal pliers, also known as wire cutters, to cut lengths of music wire and electrical wire.

A set of long-reach, ball-head hex drivers comes in very handy. Use hex drivers to tighten cap-head screws and setscrews.

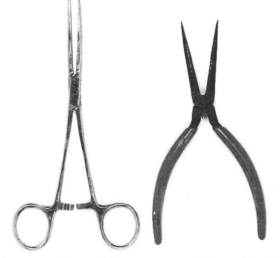

Long-nose pliers and forceps are great for reaching into tight spots to pick up or grip small items.

Required tools for building wood kits:
• hobby knife and spare blades;
• small tack hammer or a ball-peen hammer;
• 12-inch straightedge and a metal yardstick;
• box of straight T-pins;
• needle-nose or long-nose pliers;
• razor saw or hacksaw with a fine blade;
• coping saw;
• clamps, clothespins, or spring clips;
• 90-degree or combination square (or a right triangle);
• hand drill (perhaps battery-operated?);
• drill-bit set with bits ranging in diameter from $\frac{1}{16}$ inch to $\frac{1}{4}$ inch;
• set of Allen wrenches;
• regular and Philips-head screwdriver sets;
• sanding blocks and assorted sheets of sandpaper;
• heat gun and a heating iron (for applying Mylar film, cloth and other heat-shrink covering materials);

Philips-head screwdrivers—big and small—are requirements. Most servos are mounted with Philips-head screws.

To assemble straight and true, you'll need a combination square or right-angle square to check the angle.

A drill and a set of bits are required; bits in sizes of from 1/16 inch to 1/4 inch should meet most of your drilling needs.

Additional tools—nice to have but not absolutely required:
• drill press;
• set of taps, including 4-40, 6-32, 8-32, 10-32 and 1/4-20 sizes and a tap holder;

Use a hobby saw to cut thick pieces of balsa or stick stock such as spars and longerons. A piece broken off a hacksaw blade is a good tool for getting into tight places. Use the hobby saw with a miter box when you want to cut precise angles.

Hand-held, electric, rotary-power tools are great for drilling holes, grinding holes in plastic and cutting off thick pieces of metal. The Dremel Moto-tool is a great workbench accessory.

Carbide cutter bits such as these from Robart will pay for themselves the first time you use them. Chucked in a Moto-tool, they cut quickly and will last a long, long time.

• carpenter's block plane and a modeler's razor plane;
• band saw or jigsaw (or both!);
• disk sander and belt sander;
• hand-held Dremel Moto-tool with associated grinding, cutting and sanding bits;
• small metal hobby lathe;
• air compressor and spray-gun painting set;
• airbrush painting set.

I can't be without a belt sander, but you really don't need one to make great-looking models.

You don't have to have a drill press, but it's very nice to have. The table is adjustable, as is the spindle speed. The press can be used as a drill, a sander—even as a vertical lathe with the proper fixtures.

You'll find a band saw very useful, but it isn't absolutely necessary. Such saws can be free standing like this one or smaller, bench-top models; either type will pay for itself in no time.

Glues are available in many types for their many applications. Knowing which type to use and where helps you build a strong airplane (see text).

If you buy these tools gradually over the years, your initial outlay won't be excessive, and they'll really add value to your workshop. Holidays and birthdays are ideal times to request such items!

The other supplies you'll need may be divided into four groups: adhesives, hardware, finishing supplies and replacement tools.

ADHESIVES

The three most popular are cyanoacrylate (CA or instant glue), slow- and fast-setting epoxies and aliphatic resins (yellow carpenters' glue).

• CA—comes in thick, medium and thin viscosities and is used for general assembly. You could use it to assemble an entire model if you wanted to do so. It's very strong and easy to use, and most brands come with their own spray accelerator (or "kicker") that reduces the curing time to a few seconds. Use thick or medium CA for assemblies where you apply glue to one part and then stick it to another part; use thin (penetrating) CA where two parts are

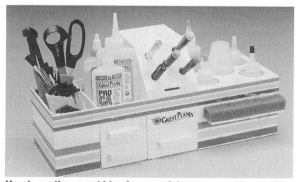

Here's another great idea for organizing your workbench. The Great Planes Bench Topper is like a workshop field box; you'll save time if you are not always looking for your tools.

brought together and the glue is run into ("wicked" into) the seam. Over time, you'll learn which type suits which jobs. Note that ordinary CA will eat into styrofoam.

Odorless CA is a good choice because its vapors do not irritate the eyes, and it does not attack foam.

Drawbacks: though CA is versatile, it is fairly expensive and many modelers have shown allergic reactions to it, particularly after repeated exposures to CA vapors. Use it in a well-ventilated area.

• Epoxies—adhesives that come in two parts and must be mixed before use. Most are very thick and very sticky; they stay where you put them and "run" very slowly, if at all.

Two-part adhesives don't dry; they cure. When the two parts are mixed in the correct proportions, a chemical reaction takes place. Epoxies are available in a variety of viscosities and curing times: 5,

If you have to remove more material than sandpaper can handle, a good modeler's plane will do the job quickly. It will breeze through shaping the leading edge and the wingtip blocks.

15, and 30 minutes as well as 1, 2 and 4 hours.

Epoxies that cure slowly offer a stronger joint because they have more time to soak deeply into the pores of the wooden pieces being bonded. Use epoxy for the firewall, landing-gear mounting plates, wing-panel attachment points and dihedral brace. A slow curing also gives you more time to make sure that parts are properly aligned and exactly where you want them.

Drawbacks: though epoxy is very strong, it is also the heaviest adhesive, so use it only where you have to (you want to minimize your model's overall weight). And again, some modelers can develop allergic reactions to epoxy; try not to have it contact your skin, and use it in a well-ventilated area.

• **Aliphatic resins**—yellow glues (Elmer's Titebond, Wilhold and Pica Gluit, etc.), are the most commonly used glues. They're inexpensive, almost odorless and will set up (dry) in only a few hours. Most aliphatic resins are water-based so may be cleaned up easily with a damp cloth or paper towel. Though referred to as "yellow" glues, several of the newer aliphatic glues are white. Don't use Elmer's white glue for model building because it isn't as water-resistant as the yellow carpenters' variety.

When using aliphatic resins, you have to either weight down the parts or pin them together because the glue takes a while to dry; this is good because if you screw up a part's alignment, you can easily reposition it before it's too late.

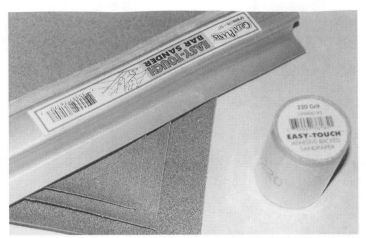

Sandpaper is available in a variety of grits to suit the many jobs it's required to do. From making surfaces smooth and ready to paint to ensuring a tightly fitting glue joint, sandpaper is a modeler's staple.

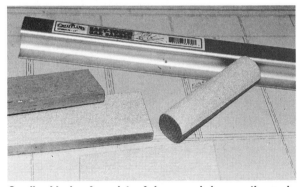

Sanding blocks of a variety of shapes and sizes are the mark of an advanced builder. Dowels, pine blocks and wedges and commercially available sanding "T" handles are all useful tools.

When building traditional, balsa and plywood airplanes, I use all these adhesives to take full advantage of their differing properties. I use CA to assemble most of a wing structure, but I switch to aliphatic resin to attach the wing's leading- and trailing-edge sheeting.

• **Specialty glues**. Certain glues do not fall neatly into one of the three basic groups mentioned above. Pacer's Zap-a-Dap-a-Goo, PFM from IMP and other "Goo" glues are all quite useful. These thick, clear adhesives seem to stick to everything—glass, steel, plastic, fiberglass and plywood. You can even use them to glue servos into fiberglass fuselages and never have to worry about the servo's coming off. But when you want to remove the servo, a sharp

knife and some effort should do the job.

I use Goop to install fuel tanks; it sticks very firmly to the slick plastic most fuel tanks are made of, and if you lay down a very thick layer of it to set the tank into, it will damp vibration fairly well.

One of the very best glues for attaching clear plastic canopies is a white glue known generically as canopy glue. It dries very clear and stays rubbery while it securely holds smooth plastic such as butyrate, styrene, ABS and vinyl. It's made by several companies, including Pacer Technology (Formula 560), Wilhold (R/C-56) and J&Z Products (Super R/C Z 56).

If you use this type of glue, you do not have to cut away your covering material to ensure a good bond. It will happily bond the canopy directly to your covering.

Another type of specialty glue is what I refer to as a "filled" epoxy. Carl Goldberg Models' Epoxy Plus is a good example: it is extremely thick and rather opaque, much like smooth toothpaste. It's excellent for gluing such materials as plywood and metal parts together, and it can also be used to make fillets.

• **Finishing resin**. Though it isn't an adhesive, I'll include finishing resin in my glue discussion. It's a thin-viscosity epoxy compound that's used to finish a model's surface. I like Pacer's Z-Poxy very much; I use it to attach fiberglass cloth to my models and to seal and fuelproof firewalls and fuel-tank compartments. Like all epoxies, it comes in two parts but is very easy to apply with a brush. You can save weight, speed application and reduce how much sanding you have to do by thinning the mixed resin with an equal amount of isopropyl alcohol. Some modelers simply pour a little finishing resin onto a fiberglass-covered wing or fuselage

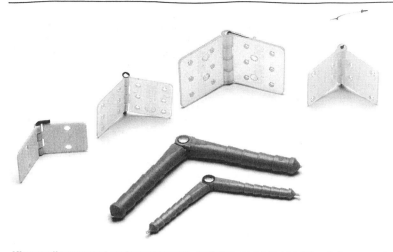

Hinges allow control surfaces to move, and they come in a variety of shapes and styles. Most are inserted into slots in the control surfaces, but the HingePoint hinges in the foreground are inserted into a hole drilled in the control surface.

• **Fasteners**—hold things together and include screws, nuts and bolts. Typical screw sizes for modeling are 2-56, 4-40, 6-32, 8-32 and ¼-20. Screw types include: self-tapping screws, sheet-metal screws, wood screws and machine screws. Nuts: common hex nuts, self-locking, or safety, nuts and blind nuts (also referred to as "T" nuts). Bolts (basically very large screws with fine threads): used for areas that require extra strength and precision; most commonly used with nuts and washers but also used with tapped holes such as in engine mounts and wing hold-down blocks.

and then squeegee the resin over its surface with a playing card or a thin sheet of balsa. Having cured, Z-Poxy is easy to sand and produces a smooth finish.

With a little experience, you'll soon develop your own glue preferences. Learn what works for you, then stick with it!

Clevises are used to attach the pushrods to the control horns that move the control surfaces. Clevises are made of plastic or metal; some come with ball-link swivels.

HARDWARE

This is, literally, the nuts and bolts of the hobby. It includes many products but may basically be divided into products that fasten, couple, move and articulate.

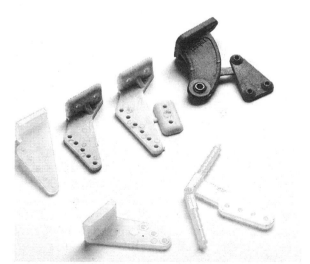

Control horns are screwed to the control surfaces and attached to the pushrod. Most kits come with pushrods and control horns as part of the hardware package.

• **Couplers**—used to bring two or more items together. In modeling, clevises join pushrods and control horns, threaded solder couplers join music-wire pushrods and clevises, and easy-connectors join pushrods and servo output wheels or arms.

• **Articulating hardware**—mainly associated with control surfaces, this includes parts such as hinges, control horns and clevises. Hinges are available in a variety of types, including the fabric or easy CA type, flat, one-piece flex hinges and pinned hinges. All these are inserted into slots cut in the control surfaces. Hinge-point-type hinges are inserted into holes drilled into the various surfaces. All hinges are glued into place, but the flat plastic type is often further secured by being cross-pinned with straight pins or toothpicks inserted through them and the control surface.

Clevises and control horns work together and are used to connect the various control surfaces to the pushrod in a way that doesn't bind when the surface is deflected. Clevises and horns may be plastic or metal and come in sizes that are specific to the size of the model being built. For safety, always match the size of your hardware to the size of the model you're building; clevises come in two sizes: 2-56 and 4-40, and they may be threaded or have to be soldered on. Threaded clevises are simply screwed onto the end of the threaded end of a wire pushrod and then secured with a jam nut. They are easy to adjust—screw them in or out—and this allows you to adjust control surfaces quickly at the flying field. Solder clevises are typically used at the servo end of the pushrod and are not adjustable. It is important to clean a freshly soldered clevis with a mild solvent to remove any leftover soldering flux. If left on the clevis and pushrod, the flux will quickly corrode the metal and affect its strength. Lacquer thinner or acetone and a small metal brush will quickly clean the solder joint and improve its looks.

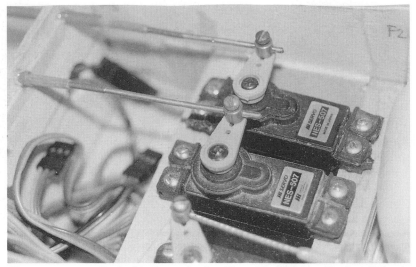
These servos are attached to the pushrods with easy connectors. The installation is quick and easily adjustable.

FINISHING PRODUCTS

There's an impressive number of products available to paint and finish your model—an almost unlimited choice for making your model look pretty.

These little brass things are commonly known as easy connectors. They're attached to servo arms and used to connect the servo arm to the pushrod.

These clamping (locking) collars keep wheels attached to music-wire axles.

You can tap threads into a hole or use blindnuts. Insert these threaded blindnut inserts into holes. The small tangs around the flange bite into the wood and prevent the blindnuts from rotating as you tighten the screw.

Such products include iron-on films and fabrics, sealants, primers and paints.

• **Iron-on films**—the quickest and most used finishing materials, they include Top Flite's MonoKote, Carl Goldberg's Ultracote, Hobby Lobby's Oracover and Coverite's 21st Century film—all Mylar plastics with a very smooth, shiny surface on one side and a heat-activated adhesive on the other. Mylar shrinks when heated and can also be stretched while it's hot. With experience, you'll be able to cover a medium-size model in about an afternoon, but if you're just starting, plan to take a weekend's worth of spare time.

• **Iron-on fabric**—painted and unpainted—is also

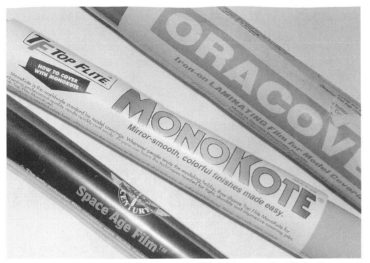

There are many types of covering material: Mylar plastic film is the most popular, and even beginners find it fairly easy to apply.

an option. Coverite makes both types, and many modelers feel that 21st Century fabric is the easiest of all to apply successfully. Some fabrics don't have the adhesive already applied, and for large models, this can represent quite a saving in weight. Sig Mfg.'s Koverall and F&M Enterprises' Stits Lite are examples of unpainted, heat-shrinkable fabric. You only apply adhesive at key points (see Chapter 8 for more on this).

• **Paint**—a more traditional finish. You must first fill and seal the wood grain to make it smooth. You can use iron-on fabric as a base for your sealant and primer coats, or try fiberglass cloth and resin, silk, silkspan, or tissue. Paint looks very attractive, but it takes longer to do and is also heavier than iron-on film.

Many coats of primer and sealant must be applied and sanded smooth between coats. Primers and sealants do not cover the wood grain; they fill its grooves. Sand each coat down almost completely before you apply the next one to minimize weight and maximize the smoothness of the surface to be painted.

Paints come in a large variety of colors and types and in spray cans. Make sure that the paint you use is fuelproof because model fuel is a mixture of nitromethane and alcohol, which will dissolve many household paints.

Aircraft dope is the oldest and most recognized model paint. It has been used since the beginning of aviation, and many modelers prefer it even though it has a strong odor and must be used with adequate ventilation. It's less opaque than most of the other paints, so you need more coats of it. Properly applied and given a final sprayed-on

Always use fuelproof model paints. Many spray paints such as these urethanes are available in colors that match covering film.

Epoxy paints are very tough and come in two parts that must be mixed to cure.

clear coat, a dope finish is a thing of beauty. Its only drawback is that it never really cures and will continue to shrink very gradually for the life of the model; years later, this can ultimately wrinkle or deform some of the model's details.

Polyurethane paints are very popular and are available from many companies. These dry quickly, cover well, resist being scuffed and will cover almost any surface, including aluminum and plastic. Polyurethane is very resistant to glow fuels.

Epoxy paints are also well suited to models, but they come in two parts that must be mixed accurately if they're to cure properly. Epoxy paints are best applied with a spray gun, and you must use the proper safety equipment: read the manufactur-

Shelves such as these offer a great way to keep nuts, bolts, screws and washers, etc., organized and within easy reach.

er's instructions and warnings when using any type of paint.

EXPENDABLE TOOLS

Certain staples are used so frequently that our stocks of them must be constantly replenished:
- masking tape;
- sandpaper;
- razor blades;
- modeling pins;
- cut-off wheels;
- saw blades, etc.

You can save a lot by buying them in bulk. Ask a modeling friend or two to join you in an order; split the cost and share the savings.

We now have a place to build and the tools to do the job; let's build something.

5
Basics of Building

Whichever type of model you choose to build—ARF, ARC, all foam, built up, or all wood—the parts required to build it will mostly be the same and will require similar—even identical—approaches to installation. All glow-powered models have an engine, engine mount, fuel tank, landing gear, radio equipment and pushrods. To successfully produce a model that flies safely, you have to assemble and install these items properly. Let's start at the front of the model and work our way back.

Figure 1 Typical engine and engine-mount installation.

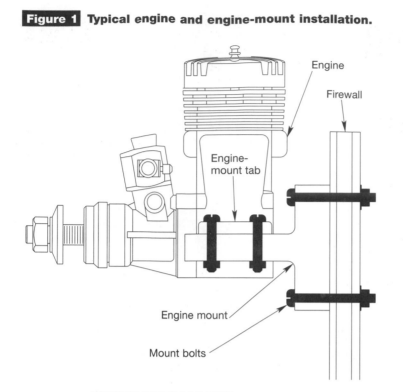

There are several types of engine mount: plastic or metal; one-piece molded mounts and separate beam mounts. The mount may even be built-in hardwood beams or made of plastic or aluminum plates (common in ARF models).

Position the engine on the mount and mark the engine's mounting-hole positions on the mount's surface; then drill all the way through the mount so the mounting bolts will pass completely through it (see Figure 1). Put a washer and a locknut on each bolt, and tighten the nuts on the bolts to hold the engine securely.

Alternatively, after marking the positions for the holes, drill holes of a smaller diameter than the bolts, and then tap them with threads that will match the bolts. I prefer this method because the bolts grip the

ENGINE INSTALLATION

When you take your new engine out of its box, you'll notice that it has a large mounting tab, or flange, on each side. Each tab has two holes (see Figure 1). These tabs match the engine mount; to securely bolt the engine into place, you will have to drill matching holes in the mount. Depending on the engine's size, you'll mount it with 4-40, 6-32, or 8-32 bolts, which you'll find in the hobby shop packaged with the appropriate washers and locknuts.

This is a hardwood-beam engine mount; the two beams are built into the fuselage structure by being epoxied into square openings in the plywood formers. Balsa blocks will be glued around the rails to give the nose of the model its shape.

This Hangar 9 Easy Fly 40 engine mount is a typical plate mount. Attach the engine to two small aluminum or plastic plates, then bolt the plates into place on the fuselage's built-in mounting rails.

tapped threads more tightly, and there is no need for locknuts on the bottom side of the engine mount. Cap-head bolts last much longer than slotted-head screws, and there's no chance of losing the nuts in the grass at the flying field because there are no nuts to lose.

If your model has hardwood engine-mount rails instead of a separate, bolt-on mount, use blind nuts for a secure engine installation.

With plate mounts, you first install the engine on the plates and then bolt the plates to the supports

This is another example of a plate engine-mounting system. In this case, the Performance Products Unlimited setup is designed to damp engine vibration and minimize its effects on the model. The engine is bolted to the middle plate.

One-piece metal and plastic engine mounts are available in several sizes to fit the variety of engines on the market. For a perfect engine/mount fit, buy a mount that has been predrilled specifically for your engine.

already installed in the model. Again, just follow the instructions, and you'll be fine.

FUEL TANK

Directly behind the firewall and the engine mount is the fuel-tank compartment. Because the tank is close to the engine, fuel doesn't have to travel far to reach it, and throttle response and engine performance

will be consistent.

Fuel tanks are generally made of tough, flexible plastic and have a rubber stopper and a cap to seal them (see Figure 2). Two (sometimes three) brass tubes pass through the stopper and are used to connect the fuel lines to the

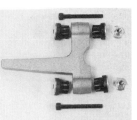

Here the soft "Iso-" vibration-damping mount (offered by Du-Bro) has been taken apart to show its several parts.

tank. Inside the tank, one of the brass tubes is attached to a flexible tube, at the end of which is a heavy, metal, pick-up fitting called a "clunk." No matter what the attitude (orientation) of your model, the clunk is always at the bottom of the tank to ensure that the fuel pick-up line can draw fuel for the engine.

A second brass tube is bent at 90 degrees, and its inside end is bent toward the top of the tank. This is the vent; it allows air to enter and leave the tank to allow the fuel to flow properly.

If a third brass tube passes through the tank's stopper, it's for a separate filling line. For the fuel

This Sullivan fuel tank has two brass tubes (vent and outlet) and a typical cap and rubber stopper seal. The screw in the middle of the cap tightens the stopper and cap.

tank to deliver fuel properly, this line must be sealed when not in use, so it's usually blocked with a threaded stopper screw.

You must use fuel tubing of the right diameter for your engine. Check the instructions; typically:

• **.15 to .25ci engines** require $3/32$-inch-inside-diameter (i.d.) tubing;

• **.40 to .60ci engines** require $1/8$-inch-i.d. tubing. If the tubing is too large, it won't fit tightly enough around the carb's fuel-inlet fitting and the tank's brass outlet tubes. It might slip off while the engine is running, or—at the very least—air might leak into the tubing and make the fuel/air mixture too lean. If the fuel tubing is too small, fuel flow will be restricted, and that will also result in poor engine performance.

Figure 2 Typical fuel-tank assembly.

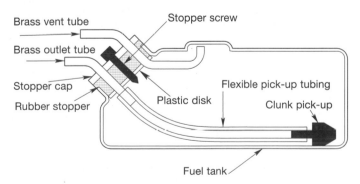

Brass vent tube
Stopper screw
Brass outlet tube
Stopper cap
Flexible pick-up tubing
Plastic disk
Rubber stopper
Clunk pick-up
Fuel tank

This illustration shows a two-tube setup consisting of a vent and an outlet tube. The vent is typically connected to the engine's muffler, and the outlet tube is connected to the carb.

Using brass tubes and fuel tubing of the correct size is important for proper fuel flow to the engine. To ensure consistent engine performance, in-line fuel filters are recommended.

• **Fuel foaming**—a vibration-caused condition in which frothy bubbles are formed in the fuel; it causes the engine to run lean and erratically. To avoid fuel foaming, you need to minimize the transmission of engine vibration to the fuel: pad the fuel tank with foam rubber padding; it's sold at hobby shops in ¼- and ½-inch-thick sheets. Simply wrap it around the tank and hold it in place with rubber bands or masking tape. Also put additional padding into the fuselage on both sides of the tank to prevent it from shifting.

In some models, the padding can be attached to the tank compartment with spray adhesive, and the tank may then be inserted into this snug foam pocket. However you do it, it prevents the fuel from foaming and thus ensures more consistent engine runs.

Figure 3 Landing-gear arrangements.

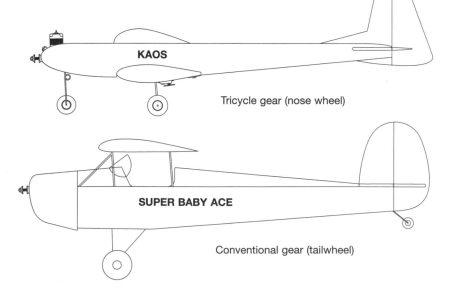

KAOS

Tricycle gear (nose wheel)

SUPER BABY ACE

Conventional gear (tailwheel)

LANDING GEAR

Except for small sport models and hand-launched gliders, all models need wheels and landing gear. Landing gear provides the necessary ground/propeller clearance, and it absorbs the shock associated with landings and high-speed ground runs. There are two basic types:

• **Conventional** (tail-dragger). Most classical and antique airplanes have conventional, or "tail-dragger," gear, and many modelers prefer its looks, even though a tail-dragger is a little more demanding on takeoff and landing. Tail-dragger pilots soon learn the critical importance of good rudder control on takeoff (see Chapter 10, "Learning to Fly").

• **Tricycle** (nose gear)—like the Cessna's. Most

A typical, music-wire landing gear. Two pieces of music wire are wrapped with copper binding wire and then soldered together at the axle area.

trainers have tricycle landing gear.

The two most commonly used landing-gear materials are sheet aluminum and steel music-wire pieces that have been bent and soldered together.

Aluminum landing gear is simple in design and very easy to install; it's usually attached to the bottom of the fuselage with four bolts. Special axle fittings are attached to the lower end of the gear, and the wheels are held on the axles with locking collars. Sometimes, the axles are simply long bolts.

Music-wire landing gear

Stay-brite silver solder (available at most hobby shops) is excellent for landing-gear assembly.

is a little more difficult to build and set up. You'll need copper wrapping wire, a propane torch and StaBrite (or similar) silver solder and flux. Kits usually include two pieces of music wire that have been bent to shape; as will be detailed in the kit's instructions, these have to be properly positioned in a wood jig (or bolted into place on the fuse-lage) and then wrapped with copper wire at the joints and soldered together. Before the joints are soldered, you must be absolutely sure that all the parts are properly aligned. Music-wire landing gear is attached to the fuselage bottom with metal or

A tailwheel assembly is much smaller than a nosewheel setup and so produces much less drag while the model is in flight. The tailwheel will later be attached to the rudder (this further simplifies the model's linkage).

plastic landing-gear straps, and the wheels are held on the axles with locking collars.

With conventional gear, the third wheel is mounted under the airplane's tail. The tailwheel assembly is mounted on a plywood base in the tail of the plane and is directly or indirectly connected to the rudder. No additional pushrod is required, and because it's smaller, a tailwheel produces less drag than a nosewheel.

The construction of tricycle gear starts at the airplane's nose. The nose gear is bolted to the firewall with a mounting bracket and the formed-wire gear is held in place with a couple of locking collars. A tiller arm is attached to the music-wire gear strut (the gear leg), and a pushrod is used to connect the

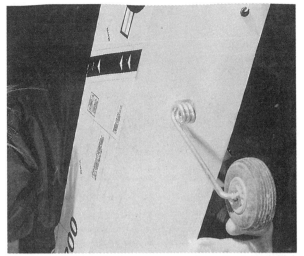

This Altech Tamecat trainer nose gear shows the typical wire coil near the top of the gear leg. The coil absorbs landing shock without transferring it to the mounting bracket in the fuselage.

nose gear to the rudder servo. The nose gear works with the rudder and provides very positive steering and good ground handling.

CONTROL LINKAGE

Control linkage transfers servo movements to the control surfaces. Every part of the control linkage must be installed in a way that permits proper control-surface throw (movement) and must operate without binding.

Let's start with the servos. At both ends of a servo's case, there's a mounting tab that allows the servo to be anchored to the airframe with servo-

Figure 4 Servo detail.

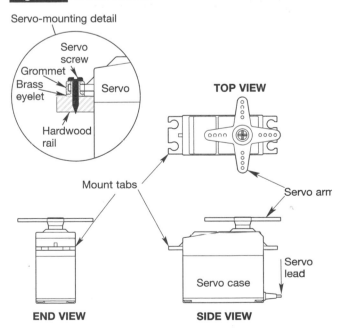

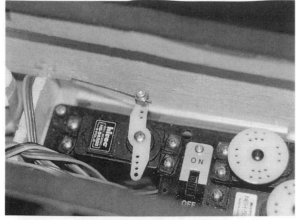

A typical throttle-servo installation. Note that a flexible steel cable in a plastic outer sleeve connects the servo to the engine's carburetor.

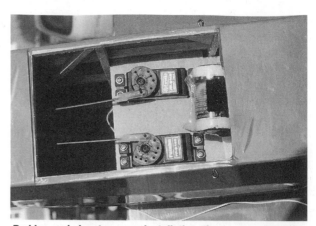

Rudder- and elevator-servo installation: the servos are mounted on a plywood tray, and the wire pushrods are attached to the servos with simple L-bends. "Keepers" securely hold the pushrods in place on the servo arms.

Installed in a Nifty 50 trainer, these flexible pushrods are supported by balsa scraps. To ensure the safe control of your model, the outer pushrod tube must be glued to the fuselage in several places (note the balsa supports).

PUSHRODS

Pushrods transmit servo action into control action; they can be either rigid or flexible.

• **Rigid pushrods**. These may be wood—solid balsa, pine or dowel—or hollow fiberglass arrow-shaft material. The pushrods' wire ends can be attached to clevises or to the servos, and there are several attachment methods: Z-bends, easy connectors, ball links and rod keepers. All allow a removable and, in some cases, an adjustable connection between the servo's output arm and the pushrod.

• **Flexible plastic pushrods**. These consist of an

mounting screws. To properly support the servos and to isolate them from engine vibration, rubber grommets and brass eyelets are inserted into the mounting tabs. When properly tightened, the servo-mounting screws compress the rubber grommets to the limit of the brass eyelets. Note that the brass eyelets are inserted into the grommets from underneath so that the flanged end of the eyelet provides a hard mount for the wood or servo tray (see Figure 4).

Most radio sets include plastic servo trays that are designed to be mounted on plywood or hardwood rails that are built into the model's radio compartment. The servo tray may also be made of thin plywood cut out to fit your servos, or the servos may be mounted directly on wooden rails. Typically, larger models have enough room for a plastic servo tray while in smaller models, the servos are mounted directly on wooden rails or trays.

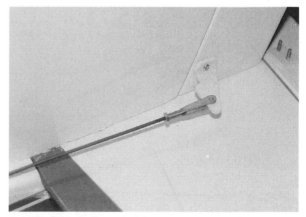

A typical clevis-to-control-horn connection. The clevis is locked into position on the control rod with a small jam nut that has been tightened against the base of the clevis.

outer tube and a narrower inner tube that slides inside it. Threaded-wire rod ends are screwed into the ends of the inner tube and are attached to the clevises or connectors. If the pushrod is to operate properly, the outer tube must be secured to the airframe in several places, and the inner tube must be able to move freely inside it. Holes are typically drilled in various formers in the fuselage and the outer tube is pushed through and then glued into these holes. In the absence of formers, you may add scrap balsa to support the pushrod.

To install the pushrods, it's best to first install the control surfaces, the control horns and the servo so that their end positions, i.e., the extent of their mechanical movement in normal operation, can be determined; then install the pushrods. Most trainers already have pushrod exit slots cut in the fuselage sides, or the instructions at least describe where they should be cut. The important thing to remember is that the pushrods should line up with the servo output arm without binding.

If there's too much space between a flexible pushrod's exit and the control horn it's connected to, you'll have too much "slop." Such slop can lead to control-surface "flutter" (a buzzing control-surface vibration in flight) that can damage your model.

WING LINKAGE

With respect to the ailerons, wing linkage typically entails some type of 90-degree change of control direction. This movement is accomplished with 90-degree bellcranks, long, gently

Figure 5 Rigid wing linkage for aileron control.

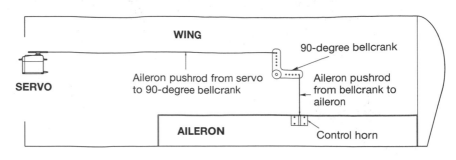

Figure 6 Flexible wing linkage for aileron control.

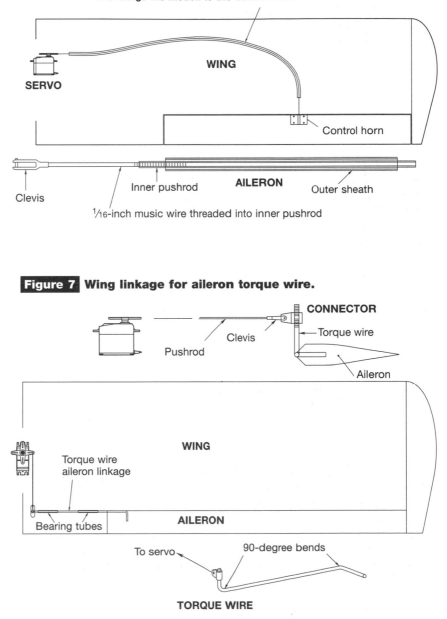

Figure 7 Wing linkage for aileron torque wire.

Figure 8 Direct-control aileron-servo setup.

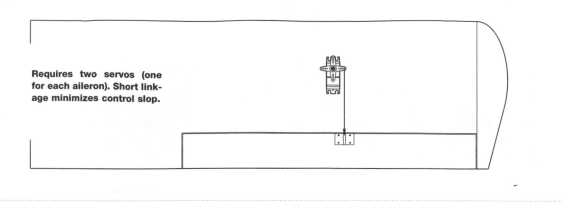

Requires two servos (one for each aileron). Short link-age minimizes control slop.

bowed flexible pushrods, or torque-wire setups (see Figures 5 through 8). Typically, the aileron servo is installed mid-wing to make it easy to connect the servo lead to the RX, which is in the fuselage under the wing. The aileron linkage is then hooked up in such a way that it moves the ailerons in opposite directions.

For a torque-wire arrangement (used on strip ailerons) two shorter pushrods are hooked to the ailerons with one pushrod attached to either side of the servo output arm (see Figure 7).

With a flexible pushrod, the rod sweeps around and is attached to the aileron control horns at a 90-degree angle (see Figure 6). One of the simplest and best aileron setups is a short control rod that connects the servo directly to the control surface (see Figure 8).

With all control-linkage setups, clevises are used to allow the system to be adjusted to some degree, and this is very important to final control trimming. Clevises can be rotated to adjust their position along the length of the pushrod. This allows mechanical centering of the control surface.

A knowledge of building basics sets the stage for our next step: building your first model.

Let's get started.

Figure 9 Control-surface motion.

Control horns allow the back and forth motion of the pushrods to be converted to control-surface motion.

Clevis

Control horn

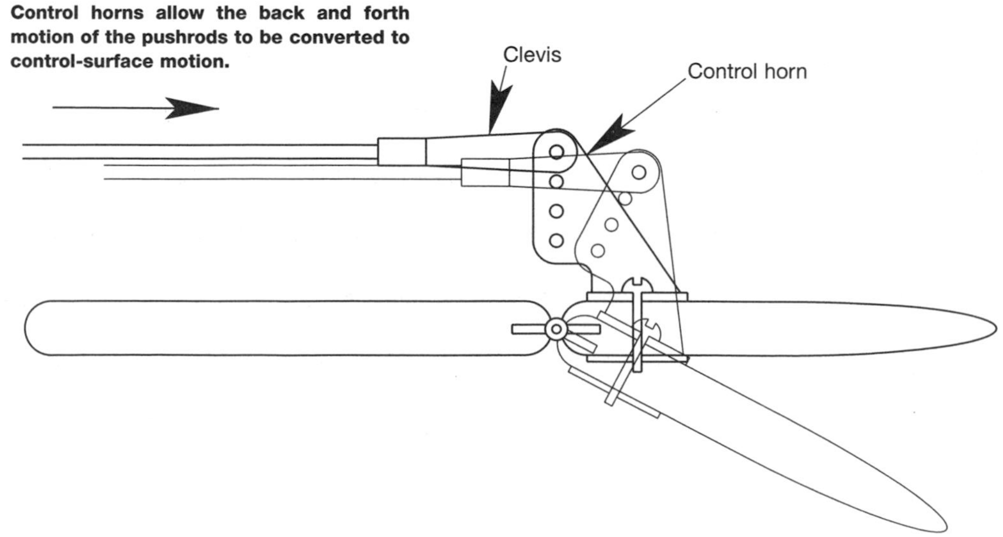

6

Building Your
First ARF Model

Well, here we are; you've decided on a first model—an almost-ready-to-fly (ARF) kit (wise choice!)—bought a radio system and an engine and have read all the instructions that came with them. You've also checked the hardware list that came with the kit and bought the parts (if any) that were specified as necessary but that weren't included with it. You have an uncluttered, well-lit building area and all the tools and supplies you need for the job. My purpose in this chapter is to show you how easy it is to build an ARF model. Let's get started.

Having made the joiner, insert it into the slot in the roots of the wing panels. It should be a snug fit, but not overly tight. There should be enough room for the epoxy; before gluing the panels together, dry-fit them to check their fit.

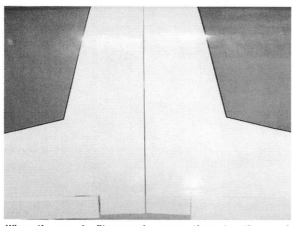

When the panels fit properly, epoxy them together, and secure the assembly with tape and a few straight pins until the epoxy has cured. If the panels do not fit together properly or if there are gaps between them, sand until they fit properly.

BUILDING AN ARF

An ARF model such as Thunder Tiger's Tiger Trainer 40, is a good place to start. It comes out of the box with most of the work already done. To put one together, you first join the wing halves, add the aileron servo and linkage and then hinge the ailerons to the wing's trailing edge (TE). Turn your attention to the fuselage: add the servo tray, and then attach the tail parts. Then install the landing gear and the engine and finish by installing the fuel tank and the radio system. Sound easy? It is!

• WING. This arrives in two halves (one right and one left) covered with a heat-shrink film and looks pretty good. The center root ribs of each wing half (or panel) are slightly angled so that when the two are glued together, you'll have the correct amount of wing dihedral (dihedral is illustrated in Figure 3 in Chapter 1). A plywood dihedral brace fits into a slot in the root ends of the wing halves. Start by gluing together the three, ⅛-inch plywood pieces that make up this ⅜-inch-wide dihedral brace.

Use 30-minute epoxy to join the brace's parts, which you should clamp together until the epoxy has cured. After that, sand the brace until it fits the slots in the wings halves nicely. Slide the wing panels together until the root ribs touch neatly, and check that the wing halves fit—no gaps. If there are gaps, separate the panels, adjust the brace and try again. When everything is OK, apply epoxy to the brace—one end at a time—and to the inside of each slot, then carefully slide the brace into position and slide the panels together. Use tape and a few straight pins to hold the panels together, and set the wing aside until the epoxy has cured. Wipe away any access epoxy with a paper towel and some isopropyl alcohol.

Once the epoxy has cured, flip the wing over and cut out the opening in the wing's center section for the plywood aileron-servo tray: glue the tray on, and then temporarily hold the servo in position. Mark the positions of the servo-mounting screws on the tray; then remove the servo, drill the screw holes in the tray with a 1/16-inch-diameter drill bit, then screw the servo permanently into place (see photos).

The ailerons come already hinged to the wing TE, but the hinges have to be glued into place. Remove the ailerons and hinges, add glue and reinstall them. A drop of oil on the hinge pins will prevent the epoxy from binding the hinges and will allow them to move freely after the epoxy has cured. To ensure that they'll operate freely, work the ailerons back and forth as the epoxy cures.

At the TE, a couple of threaded wires protrude from the bottom of the wing. These are the aileron torque wires, and you must make up the pushrods to connect them to the aileron servo's output wheel. Attach the pushrod wire to the torque wire

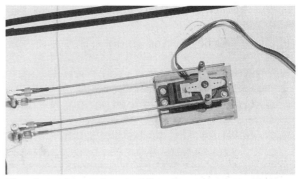

The plywood servo tray and the aileron servo are in place; note the use of "easy connectors" for the pushrod connection.

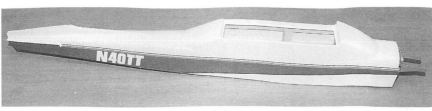

The fuselage comes out of the box completely built; its plastic top enhances its good looks.

the radio compartment.

With the servo tray in place, apply the black plastic windshields, window decals and wing-attachment dowels (use thin CA to secure the dowels).

with the small molded plastic connector that's threaded over the wire's end. The connector has a tab to which the pushrod clevis will be attached. The pushrod is attached to the servo wheel with a Z-bend or an easy connector.

Having installed the aileron linkage, make sure that the servo arm and the ailerons are centered. You can make minor adjustments with the threaded clevises. That's it for the wing—easy wasn't it? Now on to the fuselage.

■ FUSELAGE. Start by installing the plywood servo tray in the radio compartment. Test-fit the servos in the tray, then mark and drill the servo mounting screw holes as you did for the aileron servo. Use epoxy to install the tray, and be sure to install it as shown in the instructions. The larger opening in the tray is for the elevator and rudder servos while the smaller one is for the throttle servo, which should be at the front of

■ TAIL. This consists of the horizontal stabilizer and the vertical fin, both of which have to be epoxied into place on the fuselage. There are slots for the tail parts, but first, you must remove

The tail feathers come protected in a plastic bag. They come hinged, but the hinges have to be glued into place.

Glue the Tiger Trainer 40's plastic windows into place with CA or another glue that's suitable for plastics.

the covering material from the tail areas where they will be glued into place. First, trial-fit the parts into their respective slots, and use a ball-point pen to mark where covering is to be removed. Using a hobby knife, cut the film that covers the slots and remove it. Mix some 30-minute epoxy, apply it to the parts, then push them into the slots. Hold the parts with straight pins and masking tape until the epoxy has cured.

Before the adhesive cures, measure the distances from each stab tip to the fuselage side, and make sure that these measurements are equal. Then measure from the tips to a central point at the airplane's nose. These measurements must also be equal to ensure that the stab is placed squarely on the fuselage (see Figures 1 and 2). Use a square or a triangle to make sure

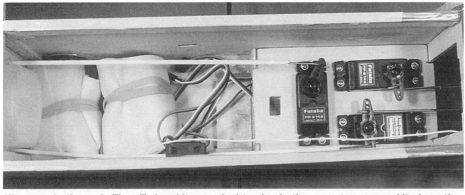

Kits vary: in the early Tiger Trainer kits, you had to glue in the servo tray; newer kits have the tray already "factory-glued" into place. Here, the radio gear has been installed and the tray is in place. The throttle servo is in front; the elevator and rudder servos are farther aft.

Figure 1 Stab position.

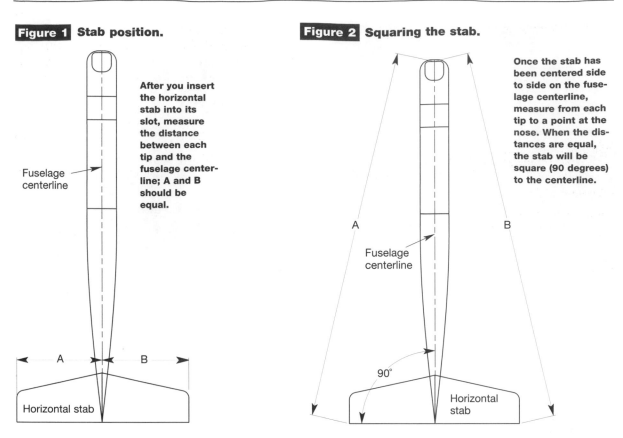

After you insert the horizontal stab into its slot, measure the distance between each tip and the fuselage centerline; A and B should be equal.

Fuselage centerline

A   B

Horizontal stab

Figure 2 Squaring the stab.

Once the stab has been centered side to side on the fuselage centerline, measure from each tip to a point at the nose. When the distances are equal, the stab will be square (90 degrees) to the centerline.

A   B

Fuselage centerline

90°

Horizontal stab

that the vertical fin is at 90 degrees to the horizontal stab (see Figure 3). Once you're happy with the parts' alignment, set the fuselage aside while the epoxy cures.

Remove the rudder and elevator from the stabs, and remove the hinges. Epoxy the hinges into place as you did with the ailerons. Having done that, install the plastic control horns.

Holding the control horns in place, mark and then drill the positions of the holes for the mounting screws. Insert these screws, and attach the horn securely with the screws threaded into the plastic

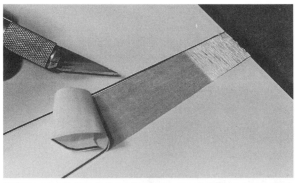

Before gluing the tail surfaces to the fuselage, you must remove the covering film from the areas to be glued to ensure a strong wood-to-wood joint.

Figure 3 Fin alignment.

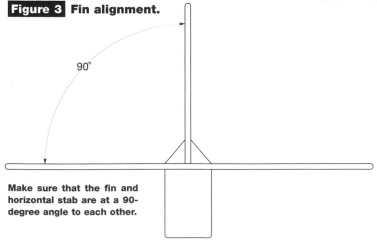

90°

Make sure that the fin and horizontal stab are at a 90-degree angle to each other.

The tail surfaces have been epoxied into place. Epoxy cures slowly, allowing you time to ensure that the surfaces and fuselage are properly aligned.

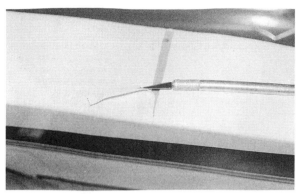

Under the film covering in the bottom of the fuselage, there is a slot for the main landing gear; cut the film away from the slot.

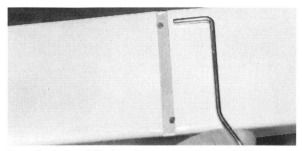

Note the holes drilled in the wooden slot block. The short, vertical, gear-wire bends go into these holes—an arrangement that locks the gear wires into place and allows them to absorb landing shock.

backing plates. Do this for both the rudder and the elevator.

■ **LANDING GEAR.** In this kit, the main gear is made of music wire and comes already bent to shape. In the bottom of the fuse, there's a slot for the main gear. Cut the covering away from the slot, and insert the short vertical parts of the gear into the holes in the landing-gear slot at either side of the bottom of the fuse. Center the metal landing-

Two metal straps and four screws hold the gear wire in the slot. The holes for the mounting screws still have to be drilled.

gear straps over the gear, and mark and drill the holes for the mounting screws. Secure the gear with the screws provided. Slip the wheels onto the gear and secure them with the supplied metal wheel collars.

■ **NOSE GEAR.** First, install the engine mount and the small landing-gear support bracket. These are simply screwed into place on the firewall. There are already holes drilled and blind nuts installed in the firewall for this. With these in place, slip the nose

In the Tiger Trainer, the engine mount and the nose-gear mounting bracket are combined. The finished installation is strong and easy to maintain.

wheel onto the nose gear and secure it with the locking collar. Also slide the tiller arm onto the gear, and then slide the gear into the support bracket and secure it with two locking collars. Finally, add the steering-control wire and its guide tube, which exits the bottom front of the fuselage.

■ **ENGINE INSTALLATION.** Mount the engine on the adjustable plastic engine mount, install the throttle linkage, and assemble and install the fuel tank (see photos).

The Tiger Trainer's instructions tell you to attach the engine to its mount by drilling four, $3/32$-inch-diameter holes and securing the engine with 3x15mm sheet-metal screws. Before you drill the mounting holes, make sure that, as mounted, the engine's thrust washer will be $4^1/2$ inches in front of the firewall.

■ **FUEL TANK.** A 10-ounce tank comes with the kit. Install the pick-up tube and clunk, and then install the stopper.

The plastic engine-cowl halves have been glued together. After that, the cowl has to be trimmed to fit the front of the fuselage. When the engine is installed, the cowl should not touch it anywhere; use a hobby knife to trim the plastic.

Figure 4 Squaring the wing.

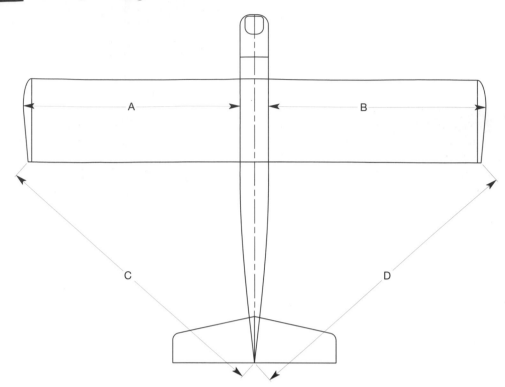

The wing is squared to the fuselage in the same way as the stab. Measure from the tips to the fuselage sides and make sure that A and B are equal. Then measure from each tip to a point at the tail. C and D should also be equal.

Attach two lengths of fuel tubing to the tank (one to the top vent and one to the fuel outlet). Slide the tank into position behind the firewall, and guide the two lengths of fuel tubing through the slot in the firewall.

With the engine, fuel tank and throttle linkage installed, it's time to install the plastic engine cowl, which comes in halves that must first be joined with a little thin CA or plastic solvent cement. It's a good idea to reinforce the seam in the cowl by gluing in a strip of fiberglass cloth with thin CA. This will strengthen the cowl. Slip the cowl over the engine, and install the muffler on the engine. Trim the cowl opening as necessary, and when the cowl fits over the engine nicely without touching it anywhere, secure the cowl to the fuselage with screws.

Connect the vent line to the muffler pressure tap, attach the fuel line to the carb, apply the cowl decals and add the prop and spinner, and you've completed the engine installation.

■ **RADIO.** This is the last thing to be installed. Hey! We've almost finished!

Position the servos in the servo tray and secure them with the mounting screws. Note that the throttle-control wire and the steering-linkage wire should line up with the servos' output arms. Hook the servo leads and an aileron extension lead to the receiver, then wrap the receiver with soft, foam-rubber padding. Install the receiver in the front of the compartment just in front of the servos, and run the two control-linkage wires above it. Plug the battery lead into the switch harness, and plug the harness into the receiver. Wrap the battery with foam and install it next to the receiver.

Assemble the rudder and elevator pushrods, cut open the pushrod exits at the fuselage tail, and install the pushrods. The pushrods are attached to the servos with Z-bends and to the control horns with clevises. The throttle- and steering-control wires are attached to the servos with easy connectors that make it easy to adjust their lengths.

Turn on the radio, center the control surfaces and the nose wheel by adjusting the length of the control linkage, and check that the control-surface throws and directions are correct.

Attach the wing to the fuselage with rubber

Before you fly:

■ Double-check the CG; is it where the instructions say it should be?

■ Check all control surfaces for freedom of movement. Do any show signs of inappropriate slop or binding?

■ Check all the screws, clevises, nuts and control horns. Did you forget to connect any? Are all the clevises secured with a safety clip or a short length of fuel tubing?

■ Is the radio equipment wrapped with foam and securely positioned in the fuselage?

■ Have you ground-checked your radio to ensure that it sends a strong signal and that your receiver is picking up control inputs?

■ Is all the fuel tubing properly connected and free of kinks?

■ Have you fully charged the onboard batteries? (depleted batteries are a common cause of model crashes).

■ Is your plane properly fueled?

■ Do any of the servo-lead wires interfere with the servo arms or the pushrods?

■ Is the antenna properly strung and uncoiled?

■ Do your servos respond properly to control inputs? (reversed servos are another common cause of crashes).

This checklist is repeated in Appendix 5. Why not photocopy that page and keep it in your field box?

bands, and check the plane's balance point (center of gravity, or CG). On this aircraft, the CG is 3¾ inches back from the leading edge of the wing. Move the battery around inside the fuselage or add lead weight to the nose until the model balances at the CG position indicated on the plan.

Control-surface throws:
• Elevator—½ inch up and down.
• Rudder—⅞ inch left and right.
• Ailerons—⅜ inch up and down.

Hey! You know what? There aren't any parts left in the box! You just built your first model!—wasn't all that hard, was it? Now all you have to do is charge the radio batteries and wait for a calm, sunny day.

WHAT ABOUT ARCS?
Almost ready to cover (ARC) models allow you some originality in deciding how your model looks. Do you like the color scheme of a Cessna 182 you saw at a local airport? Why not replicate that scheme on *your* Cessna? How about a military olive drab and dove gray paint scheme? Sounds good to me; go ahead and do it. Anything that strikes your fancy is fair game. The only catch is that you'll have to buy the covering film and a covering iron, but we'll talk about this in Chapter 8.

BOLT-TOGETHERS
The newest kids on the block are the no-glue-required, bolt-together models. Their parts were designed to be secured with a few screws or bolts. You still have to install the engine, radio and hardware, but the hinges are already glued into place.

Some manufacturers also offer models in which the servos and engine have been installed at the factory. There has never been a better time to get into R/C! Check out the selection at the local hobby store, and if you're short of time, choose the bolt-together aircraft that you find most appealing!

BUT FIRST ...
Trainers are intended for beginners, but an experienced modeler (your instructor buddy) should check your model to make sure everything has been set up correctly. Let's pretend we're at the flying field. Pilots of full-size aircraft wouldn't dream

of taking off without a preflight inspection, and neither should you. As you complete your model in your workshop, keep these final checkout steps in mind, and you'll be better prepared for the field.

When you've completed your kit, run through the checks in this list, and when you reach the flying field, you will be much better prepared.

Building with Wood

We've discussed ARFs (almost-ready-to-fly models), ARCs (almost-ready-to-cover models) and the new bolt-together models—all good starting points; but if you enjoy building with wood—from a kit or from scratch—more is involved. There's nothing mysterious about building a wooden kit, and it isn't more difficult; it just takes longer. In fact, compared with the wooden kits of years ago, today's kits are a breeze to build. In many, the parts are designed to slip together and lock—commonly referred to as "tab-lock" construction. Others have precisely formed, laser-cut parts. With their well-written, clearly illustrated instructions, these kits take only a few weeks of work. Let's make some sawdust!

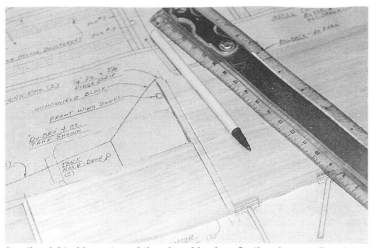

Lay the right side on top of the plan side view. On the plan, small register marks show the positions of the four fuselage formers. Transfer these marks to the fuselage side.

BUILD AN ALL-WOOD KIT

When you open the box, you'll see a lot of wood-ribs, sheeting, sticks and blocks-some hardware and perhaps a plastic cowl and wheel pants.

Roll out the plan, and you'll see two views of the fuselage—a side view and a top view—showing the positions of the firewall, the formers and the model's other details. There's usually a top view of the wing and the horizontal stabilizer, the various parts of each sub-assembly are identified, and details for other parts are often called out.

BASIC TOOLS AND SUPPLIES

- Hobby knife and extra no. 11 blades.
- Steel ruler.
- Ballpoint pen.
- Sandpaper and a sanding block.
- Adhesives (30-minute epoxy and CA).
- Hand drill and drill bits (³⁄₁₆ and ⅛ inch).
- Covering iron.

I chose a glow-powered Nifty Fifty by Florio Flyer Corp. to illustrate the building process, but the choice is yours; ask the manager of your local hobby shop to recommend a good wooden "trainer" kit. They're all built in much the same way. Note that the steps outlined in this chapter may vary from those in your instructions if you have a different kit. In any case, you'll find useful hints and tips in this chapter if you are new to building wood kits.

To complete the Nifty Fifty, you'll need to buy:
- 4-ounce Du-Bro fuel tank.
- 7 cloth hinges.
- Pair 2½-inch wheels.
- Pair ⅛-inch wheel collars.
- Set of pushrods (Sullivan Nyrod or equivalent).

- 3 clevis links.
- 3 pushrod/servo connectors.
- 2 control horns.
- 4, ⅛-inch Du-Bro landing-gear mount straps.
- 4 engine-mounting bolts (typically, 4-40).
- 2, 6-foot rolls of covering film.
- Roll of foam wing-saddle tape.
- Tailwheel bracket.

Read the instructions and identify all the parts (check to verify that they're all there). Before you start, have the radio, engine, fuel tank and the other hardware items you'll need on hand.

Roll out the plan and cover it with household wax paper, clear plastic, or Mylar film (you may use food wrap, or the backing sheet that comes with MonoKote film covering). Using masking tape, tape the transparent clear covering over the plan on your building board to protect it from glue, etc.

Ready? Let's start to build a Nifty Fifty.

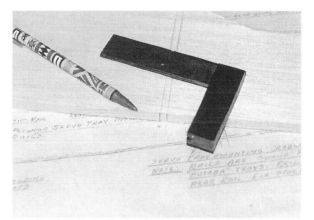

To transfer the former locations from the right to the left fuselage side, first mark the edges of the right fuselage side and then place the left side on top of the right side. Now, transfer the marks to the unmarked fuselage edges, and then draw the former position lines for the inside faces of the fuselage sides using the edge marks as a guide.

■ **FUSELAGE.** Glue the fuselage sides to the cabin-riser parts to make the fuselage's left and right sides. Referring to the plans, join the parts with CA. Having glued the sides together, mark the formers' positions on the inside of each side piece (see photo sequence). Formers (also known as bulkheads) are wooden pieces that support the fuselage top, side and bottom pieces—part of the fuselage's internal structure.

Place the left fuselage side over the plans, and mark the top and bottom edges exactly where the

Before gluing the formers to the fuse sides, mark and drill the holes for the pushrods. The Nifty Fifty has their positions shown on the plan. Other wooden models have a large hole in the center of the formers to allow the passage of the pushrods.

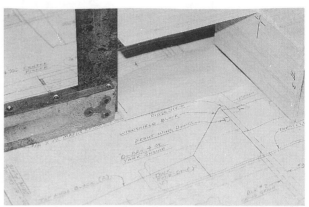

After gluing formers 3, 4 and 5 to the right side, flip this side over, and place it and the formers over the left side. Make sure the two sides are aligned properly before you glue the formers to the left side. When everything is lined up, tack-glue the formers into position.

formers will be mounted. If you mark the edges instead of the inside of the sides, you'll be able to stack the fuselage sides and transfer the marks directly to the top and bottom edges of the second side. Using a steel ruler, connect the marks along the inside surface of the sides, and mark a left and

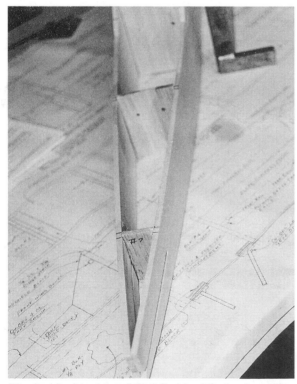

After the glue has set, pull the tail ends of the fuselage sides together; if you glued the formers into place properly, the ends will line up. If you didn't, break the tack-glued joints free and reposition the formers. When everything is aligned, glue the tail ends together. Having done this, install formers 6 and 7. Check that the fuselage is straight, and if everything is in alignment, go over all the glue joints with more glue and then set the fuse aside so the glue can fully cure.

a right fuselage side. Double-check the fuselage side view on the plan to make sure that the lines for the former locations are in the correct positions. Before gluing the formers into place, drill the holes for the control pushrods. The plans show where these holes should be drilled.

Tack-glue formers 3 and 5 into place on the inside surface of one side with a few drops of CA (see Figure 1). Use a 90-degree square to make sure the formers are square to the side. When you're sure everything lines up properly, glue the formers into their respective positions against the inside surface of the fuselage side you just positioned (see Figures 1 and 2). It's a lot like making a box. When the glue has set, lift the fuselage off the workbench and pull the tail ends together (see Figure 3). If you aligned the formers correctly when you glued the two sides together, the tail ends should line up

The Nifty Fifty has hardwood engine-mount rails. The notches in formers 1 and 2 must be cut so that the rails are the correct distance apart to accommodate your engine. Be sure to cut the notches so that the rails fit snugly and are centered on the fuselage centerline.

Figure 1 Fuselage assembly.

Figure 2 Fuselage side assembly.

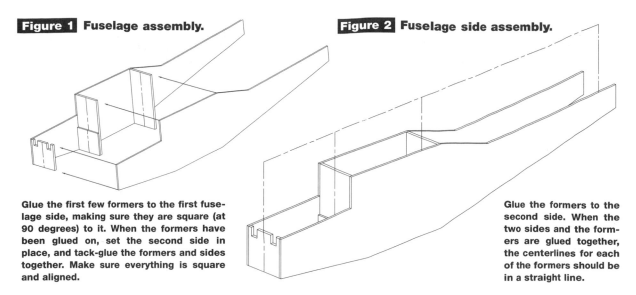

Glue the first few formers to the first fuse-lage side, making sure they are square (at 90 degrees) to it. When the formers have been glued on, set the second side in place, and tack-glue the formers and sides together. Make sure everything is square and aligned.

Glue the formers to the second side. When the two sides and the formers are glued together, the centerlines for each of the formers should be in a straight line.

within 1/16 inch or so without much trouble. If they don't, break the tacked glue joints loose and try again. When everything is aligned properly and the fuselage looks straight when viewed from the tail, glue the tail ends together, and run a bead of glue along each former's side joint.

Now install formers 4, 6 and 7. Check their positions carefully before gluing them permanently into place.

Formers 1 and 2 will be installed next, but you will have to check the notches in each former to ensure that the hardwood engine rails used in this design will fit your engine. You might have to cut the sides of the notches in these formers to allow your engine to fit between the rails precisely. As you proceed, make sure that the bottom edge of former 2 is flush with the bottom edge of former 3. Next, glue former 1 between the front edges of the two fuselage sides, making sure that its top edge

After the glue has set, use a sanding block to smooth the bottom of the fuselage so the edges of the sides and formers are flush.

and face are flush with the top and front edges of the fuselage sides. Now, using the plans for reference, glue the plywood landing-gear mount plate and the two maple engine-mount rails into place.

Next, position and trial-fit the two wooden engine-mount dampers into place (these fit under the rails and strengthen the assembly). If they fit properly, glue them into place and sand them flush with the bottom of the fuselage.

Glue the plywood tailskid brace into place, and then glue the bottom sheeting to the fuselage. Note that the sheeting's grain goes across the width of the fuselage (cross-grain). Cut the sheeting slightly oversize and then glue it

Figure 3 Fuselage side assembly.

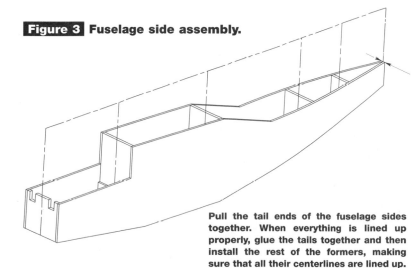

Pull the tail ends of the fuselage sides together. When everything is lined up properly, glue the tails together and then install the rest of the formers, making sure that all their centerlines are lined up.

Glue the bottom sheeting to the fuselage. Note that the grain goes across the width of the fuselage. Leave the edges of the bottom sheeting a little oversize so it overhangs the sides a bit. When all the sheeting has been glued on, trim the sheeting flush with the sides.

Two cradle sheets have to be glued to the inside of the radio compartment. Use your servo tray as a guide to cut the notches for the mounting rails in the cradle's top edge.

into place. Once the glue has dried, sand it flush with the fuselage sides. Do not glue on the top sheeting just yet; install the pushrods before doing that.

Find the two servo-tray cradles and note that their top edges are notched. These notches support the mounting rails to which you screw your servo tray. Make sure that these notches are the right distance apart so that the rails will accept your servo tray. Now glue the rails into place in the notches, making sure they're flush with the top of the cradle. Now temporarily install your servo tray, rudder and elevator servos.

See how the servo tray sits on rails in notches in the cradle? The tray allows the easy installation and removal of the servos.

Using the plan as a guide, mark and then drill the pushrod exits at the tail. These angled holes form slots that allow the pushrods to line up with the control horns when the tail is installed.

Install the outer pushrod housings so that they exit the fuselage through the exit holes. Sand the housings slightly so that the glue will adhere to them properly and glue them into place, allowing about ½ inch of the housings to extend outside the fuselage. At the servo end, holes are made in the

The large block in front of the wing saddle forms the windshield portion of the model's outline. The U-shaped cutout at its bottom will become the tank compartment.

former next to the servo tray so that the flexible pushrod outer tube is securely mounted, and the inner pushrod lines up with the servo output arm. Now install the throttle pushrod and glue it to formers 3 and 4. With the pushrods installed and supported by scrap balsa every few inches, you can now

Two blocks are glued to the rails and former 1 to round out the model's nose. These should be flush with the top of the rails and should butt up against the front of the fuselage sides.

Two smaller, tapered blocks are used to finish the front of the model. Here, the engine has been set into place, the blocks have been carved and sanded to shape, and the fuel tank has been installed.

To install the engine, first mark the positions of the mounting holes with a pencil. The engine's position is not critical, but it should not rest against former 1. Drill the holes in the mounting rails and bolt the engine into place.

complete the fuselage top sheeting, again running the grain across the fuselage width. Glue the windshield block into place, and then the four nose blocks that form the front of the fuselage. Finish the fuselage by adding the ridge strip, the front and rear saddle bars and the wing hold-down dowels (see plan).

■ TAIL FEATHERS. The horizontal and vertical stabs are made of 3/16-inch balsa sheet. Find the stab parts, glue them together, and sand them using a flat surface (sanding block). Sand the LE and TE, rounding them off nicely, as shown in the plans. Note that the elevator halves have a notch in their LEs. This is where the joiner dowel is glued to join the two halves. Cut the joining dowel's length so that when it's inserted, the tips of the elevators line up with the tips of the horizontal stab. Glue the dowel into place with epoxy and then sand everything smooth.

■ WING. The wing is built in halves, and when each has been built, they are joined to form the

wing. Start by laying the wing plan down on the workbench and covering it with wax paper. Find and then pin into place the 1/16-inch front bottom wing sheeting. Make sure it is lined up with the center of the wing on the plan. Next, using thin CA, glue the 1/4x5/8-inch leading edge to the front

When the pushrods and top sheeting have been installed, add the tail surfaces. Two small triangular pieces of balsa glued on either side of the fin complete the top sheeting.

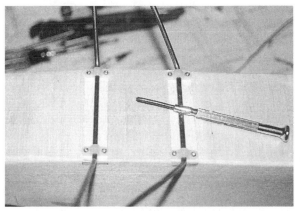

Put the landing-gear wires on top of the mounting plates, and then attach them with plastic landing-gear brackets. Solder the gear wires together at the axles, then install the tailwheel.

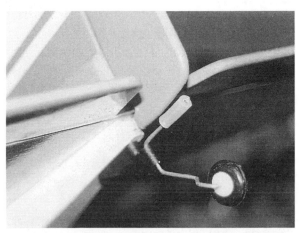

Install the tailwheel bracket so that the tiller wire is just under the rudder. A length of fuel tubing and then a metal strap will secure the tailwheel to the rudder.

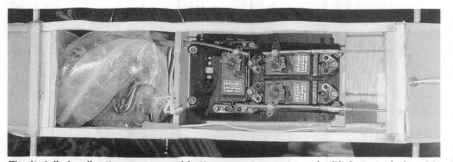

The installed radio: the receiver and battery have been wrapped with foam and placed in front of the servo tray.

This engine installation is simple and easy to adjust. Note the fuel tubing that's connected to the muffler; it provides pressure to the fuel tank for consistent engine running. The tank is behind the engine.

edge of the sheeting. Now position the wing bottom center sheeting and glue it to the LE sheeting. You have to trim the center sheeting to size to make the TE sheeting fit correctly into place. Follow this with the bottom TE sheeting, and glue it to the center-section sheeting. Note that the center-section sheeting obscures your view of the ribs on the plan. You need to draw these rib positions on the sheet-

ing so you'll be able to glue the ribs into place correctly. When all the bottom sheeting is in place over the plans, install the bottom 1/4x1/16-inch rib cap-strips as shown in the photos. Cut them to length, and glue them into place. Except for the single center rib, which is 1/8 inch thick, the ribs are all 1/16 inch thick. Note that the rib notches have a rounded interior shape (they were milled out with a router). These have to be trimmed with a razor knife so that the 1/4-inch-square spars will fit snugly into place. Now position the spar on the LE sheeting, and place a rib on the spar that's nearest to the center of the wing. Don't glue the rib

Start constructing the wing by stacking the ribs on top of one another. Check to see that they are all of the same length and width. Line up all the spar notches, pin the ribs together, then true them with a sanding block.

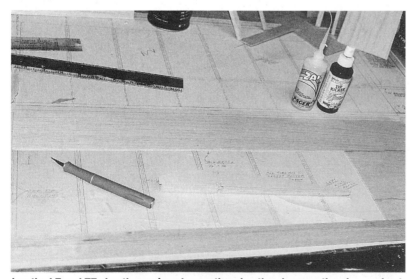

Lay the LE and TE sheeting and center-section sheeting down on the plan, and cut it to length. Glue the sheeting pieces together with thin CA and hit them with CA kicker.

to the spar yet. Slide the rib up against the LE, and glue it to the LE while keeping it properly aligned with the plan. Put the next rib into place on the spar, and glue this one to the LE, too. Work your way out to the tip until you've glued all the ribs to the LE. Now glue each of the ribs into place over the TE sheeting, making sure they're all lined up with the plan.

Note that almost all the ribs are centered over the bottom cap-strips (these are the strips of thin balsa that reinforce the edges of the ribs); the tip rib is placed flush with the strips' outer edge. Now go ahead and glue the spar to the

After, the bottom center sheeting has been glued to the LE and TE sheeting, mark the center-section sheeting where the ribs will be glued.

the dihedral template, do the same at the root end of the panels. The panels are now ready to be joined. Place the ¼-inch-thick balsa spar joiner between the two spars of one panel; next, mate the two panels by sliding the joiner between the spars of the second panel. Check that the joint between the panels is clean and tight; if it isn't, trim the panels until the fit is precise. Next, glue the joiner to the spars of each panel. Glue the end points of the LEs together as well as the respective root edges of the bottom sheeting. Position and install the front plywood dihedral brace, and glue it to the back of the LE. Find the ⅛-inch-thick center rib, cut it into front and rear sections and glue

ribs, and glue the ribs to the front bottom LE sheeting. Next, install the top spar in the tops of the ribs, making sure it is flush with the ribs' top edges. Glue the spar into place and remove the panel from the board. Repeat this process for the second wing panel. When the wing halves are at the same stage of completion, refer to the tip-angle template shown on the plan, and cut the spars and the LE to the correct angle. Referring to

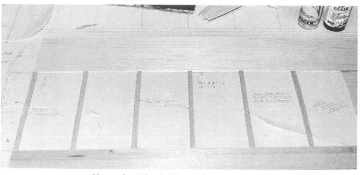

Now glue the bottom rib capstrips into place between the LE and TE sheeting.

them into place. Now add the pieces that make up the top sheeting to the wing in the same order as you added those that form the bottom sheeting. That is, first add the top LE sheeting followed by the center section sheeting and then the TE sheeting. Also install the tip sheeting, using the plan as a guide. Note that the wingtip's outline is formed by the shape of the top sheeting. Add the top rib capstrips. Finish the wing construction by adding the bottom wingtip sheeting. Sand the underside of the wingtip with a sanding block to true up all the

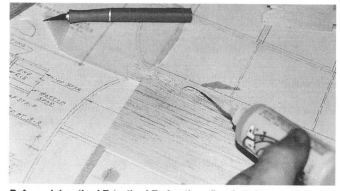

Before gluing the LE to the LE sheeting, first butt it up against the sheetings' front edges. Make sure that the LE is square with the sheeting.

Using the ribs as spacing guides, glue the bottom spar into place on top of the bottom sheeting. Do not glue the center rib into place yet; it will have to be angled inward when the two wing halves are glued together.

When all the ribs have been glued into place, you can glue the top spar into the rib notches. When the glue has set, use a sanding block to sand the top spar flush with the tops of the ribs.

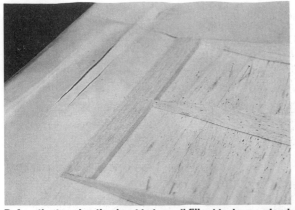

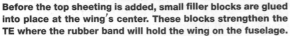

Before the top sheeting is added, small filler blocks are glued into place at the wing's center. These blocks strengthen the TE where the rubber band will hold the wing on the fuselage.

Sand the ends of the ribs with a sanding block so they taper evenly into the bottom TE sheeting. This will allow you to make a smooth, straight TE.

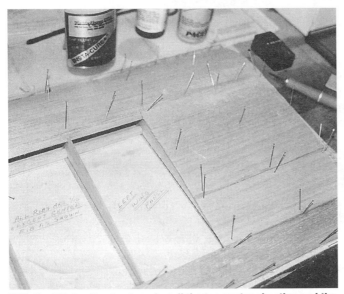

With the TE sheeting in place, install the top center sheeting and the top LE sheeting. Use aliphatic-resin glue and plenty of straight pins.

The top capstrips have been installed. You can speed construction by spraying the top of the ribs with kicker and running a bead of CA along the bottom surface of the capstrips. Hold each capstrip in place with your finger for a few seconds, and then go on to the next.

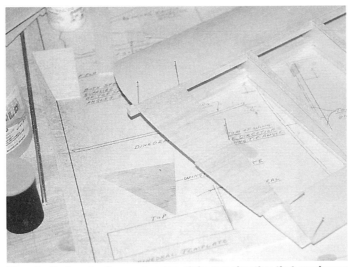

The wingtip is actually an extension of the top sheeting that overhangs the tip rib.

edges and the ends of the spars; after that, glue the precut tip sheeting into place. Sand the entire wing smooth with sandpaper and fill any gaps between the top and bottom sheeting with wood filler or putty for models. Before covering the wing, add a 1-inch strip of fiberglass cloth to its center joint, using a slow-setting epoxy. Once the epoxy has cured, lightly sand the cloth, and your wing is finished.

FINAL ASSEMBLY

Place the wing on the fuselage, and center it in the wing saddle. Slide the horizontal stab into the tail slot, and sight over the wing to see whether the tail is aligned with it. With everything properly lined up, glue the stab into place with thin CA. Remove the wing

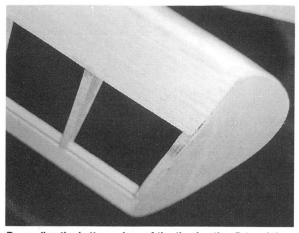

By sanding the bottom edges of the tip sheeting flat and then adding a sheet of balsa, you strengthen the tips. Make sure that the sheeting is sanded flush with the wing's top and bottom.

The completed left wing panel. Repeat the process for the right panel, and then join the panels with the plywood dihedral brace. Sand everything smooth, and you're ready to cover.

and add the vertical fin. Trial-fit the fin, and when everything looks right, glue it into place. Now you can finish the rest of the fuselage sheeting.

Sand the fuselage smooth, fill any gaps or dents and sand smooth again. All that's left to do before you cover the model is to paint the interior of the fuel-tank area and the engine compartment with thinned epoxy.

After covering the model, attach the landing-gear wires to the fuselage and then bind together and solder the front and rear landing-gear wires at the wheel axles (check your kit's instructions for the details). Add the wheels and wheel collars, and you've finished the gear.

Cut the slots in the fin and stab for the hinges and install cloth-type hinges (see the plan for hinge locations). Insert and glue the wing hold-down-dowels and the tank hold-down dowels after you've covered the fuselage (see the next chapter for tips on covering), then install the wire tailskid (or tail-

wheel assembly—your choice), and your fuselage is complete.

Bolt the engine into place on the mount rails and position the tank, holding it in place with a couple of rubber bands. Install the radio equipment. Connect the pushrods to the servos and connect the throttle linkage to the engine. Secure the wing with some rubber bands and check the model's balance (CG).

The plan shows the CG $3\frac{1}{4}$ inches back from the wing's leading edge. If you need to, move the radio or add weight until the model balances at this point (with an empty fuel tank). The instructions don't recommend control throws, but for a beginner, I suggest:

• elevator—$\frac{3}{8}$ inch up and down;
• rudder—$\frac{3}{4}$ inch left and right.

Congratulations! The kit box is empty and you have a beautiful, all-wood model airplane!

8

Covering and Finishing

I f you want to build an all-wood airplane, you'll need to learn how to finish it with a plastic film or cloth covering; it's a basic skill that will also come in handy when you need to repair a damaged aircraft, whether you built it yourself or bought it assembled.

Paint offers an alternative to using iron-on, heat-shrink cloth or film, but it's an involved process that can be nearly as much work as building the airframe. Because this is a "getting started" book, I'll discuss the easier, iron-on-film-covering process. Available in many colors, film is easier to apply than paint, and it has none of its offensive fumes or odors. But whether you choose to finish your model with paint or film, the first step is always to prepare the wood. No finishing technique will hide poor building.

To apply iron-on film coverings, you'll need a covering iron—available from many companies and in a variety of sizes and shapes.

A heat gun is another useful covering tool; use it to blow hot air over the covering film to shrink it. Be careful! It is easy to melt a hole in the film with such a gun.

To properly apply iron-on covering, you have to set the iron to the appropriate temperature. This little thermometer offers a good way to check your iron's temperature. Notice the dark color of the iron's shoe; it has seen a lot of models!

PREPARATION

■ SANDING AND FILLING. To obtain a smooth final finish, you need a smooth base. For the finish to look its best, the model must be built as perfectly as it can be. It is much better to have an average-looking finish on a superior base than to have a superior finish on an average base.

Close your eyes and feel your model with your fingertips. Are there any rough spots? How about raised seams between balsa sheets? Dents and dings must be filled and sanded smooth. The biggest difference between a good-looking model and a great

one is ... sandpaper! Start by going over the entire model with 150-grit sandpaper, and then use a tack cloth to wipe off the dust. Sand in a well-ventilated area and avoid inhaling sawdust.

Sand any raised seams until they are flat, and sand (and fill, if necessary) all the obviously rough spots. Now break out that can of model filler and fill any depressions, no matter how tiny. To help the filler material to bond, first wet the wood slightly. When the filler is dry, sand with 150-grit sandpaper and again use the tack cloth. Now repeat with 220-grit paper, and follow with 320-grit paper (the higher the number, the finer the sandpaper). If necessary, apply more filler material and wipe the model down once more with that tack cloth.

If extra CA or another glue accidentally gets "gooped" and dries on your airplane's surface, you'll often find it difficult to remove. The problem is that the balsa around the glue is softer and can therefore be removed more easily than the glue—all the more reason to take care while you build.

■ PRIMER PREP COAT. Having completed the first stage, you now have a choice: simply start covering the model, or apply one coat of a balsa prep such as Coverite's Balsarite. This seals the balsa and reduces the likelihood of wrinkles forming after the model has been covered. If you apply a prep coat, allow it to soak into the wood, let it dry completely, then lightly sand with 320-grit paper.

You'll need:
• Film or cloth-based covering material (the same or most techniques apply to both).
• Hobby knife and a lot of blades.
• Covering iron.
• Covering thermometer to check the iron's temperature.
• Yardstick or metal straightedge.

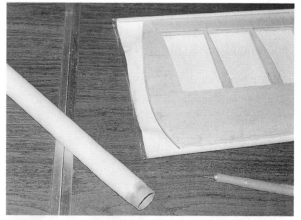

Roll out the covering and put the wing half on top of it. Cut the film about 1 inch larger than the wing all around. This extra margin gives you something to pull on when you apply the film and want to remove the wrinkles.

Read the instructions to learn the correct iron temperature for your covering film. Start tacking the film down at the center of the wing. Press the iron down so that a 1x⅛-inch section of the edge of the film is tacked into place at a time.

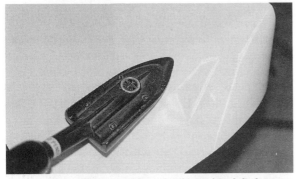

Gently pull the film toward the wingtip, and tack it down as you did at the center. Now, in a criss-crossing pattern, tack down the corners and then the centers of the edges. Work all the way around the panel until all the edges have been tacked into place.

Though it isn't vital, it's useful to have a heat gun to shrink the film; pull the material as you iron it down, and you'll eliminate all the wrinkles.

COVERING

You may choose to use a smooth film such as Top Flite's MonoKote, Carl Goldberg's Ultracote, etc., or a fabric covering such as Coverite's 21st Century

When the film has been completely tacked down around the edges, trim away the excess margin, and iron the edges down firmly.

fabric or Balsa USA's Solartex. Typically, a film looks like painted metal, and fabric imparts the antique look of doped covering. Whichever product you use, carefully read the directions it comes with.

Covering film comes in 6-foot (usual) and 15-

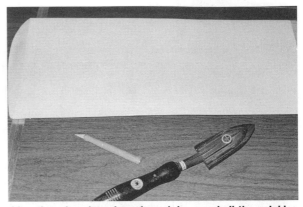

After the edges have been ironed down and all the wrinkles have been pulled out (most of them, at least!), you can shrink the film down tightly with the iron. Here, the bottom right panel has been covered.

foot rolls. An average .40 model will require about one-and-a-half 6-foot rolls. When you first examine the covering, you'll notice that it has a clear backing sheet that protects the heat-activated adhesive and prevents the material from sticking to itself. Don't remove this protective backing until you are ready to apply the film to the model.

Cover all the large surfaces first and then the pro-

Repeat the process for the next panel, and overlap the film pieces by about ¼ inch at the wing center.

gressively smaller parts in turn. This makes the best use of the material and minimizes waste. The largest surface is the wing, so we'll start there.

■ **WING.** We'll cover the wing halves with four separate pieces of film—two for the bottom surfaces and two for the top. This method allows us to cope with the wing's dihedral, and it minimizes wrinkling. The wing's center seam can easily be covered

Figure 1 Covering the wing.

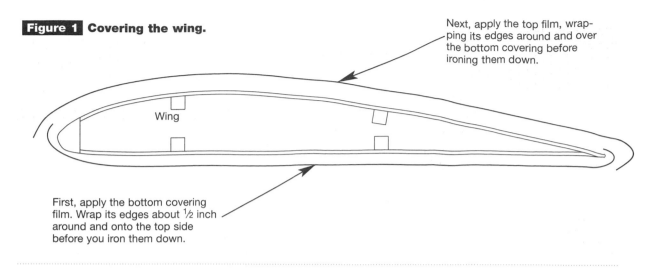

Next, apply the top film, wrapping its edges around and over the bottom covering before ironing them down.

Wing

First, apply the bottom covering film. Wrap its edges about ½ inch around and onto the top side before you iron them down.

with trim or simply left as is.

Roll out enough film to cover the bottom of one wing half plus 1 inch extra all the way around (see Figure 1). You'll hold and pull on this film "border" when you apply the film. Now set your covering iron at the recommended temperature and wait for it to heat up. Wipe the wing down again with a tack cloth to remove any dust, and then remove the protective backing from the film and lay it on one wing half's bottom surface. Smooth the film out and lightly tack it down along a 1-inch-long section of the inside edge of the wing's center. Lightly pull the film toward the wingtip and tack its outer edge down at the wingtip center (again, about a 1-inch section). Now, criss-crossing from the LE to the TE, lightly tack down a 1-inch section at the front of the center section, and then move to the wingtip TE and tack the film down there (see Figure 2).

Next, tack down the center TE and, finally, the wingtip LE. As you tack the film down, gently smooth out the wrinkles. Do the same at the wingtip and the wing root until all the edges have been tacked down. If you accidentally pull up any part of the film, simply pull it tight and

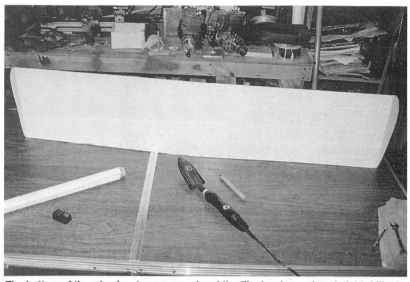

The bottom of the wing has been covered and the film has been shrunk tight. I like to iron the film down onto all the wooden "contact points."

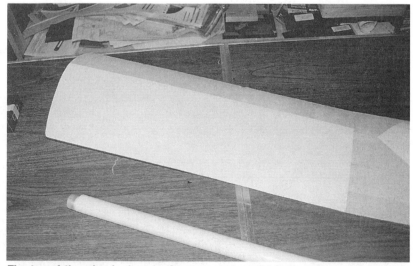

The top of the wing is done in the same way as the bottom. Here, I'm covering only the open bay area with white. I'll add a darker trim color to the LE and the center section.

GETTING STARTED IN RADIO CONTROL AIRPLANES **73**

Using a trim color at the wing's center section helps to hide the seam; the LE has yet to be covered.

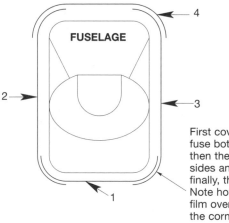

The finished wing; see how the pinstriping tape enhances the model's appearance?

reattach it.

Finally, run the iron around the wing's perimeter to fully seal down the film's edges. Trim the film's edges and iron them down firmly.

Now, starting in the center of the wing half, lightly run the iron over the film to tighten it and remove any wrinkles. Hey, it looks pretty good; now do the same for the other wing half.

With the bottom of the wing halves covered, it's time to cover the top surfaces. Because the wing's upper surface is more curved than its bottom one, it may take a little more work to get all the wrin-

Figure 3 Covering the fuselage.

First cover the fuse bottom, then the two sides and, finally, the top. Note how the film overlaps at the corners.

Figure 2 Covering the wing.

Cut the film about 1 inch oversize all around the first wing panel.

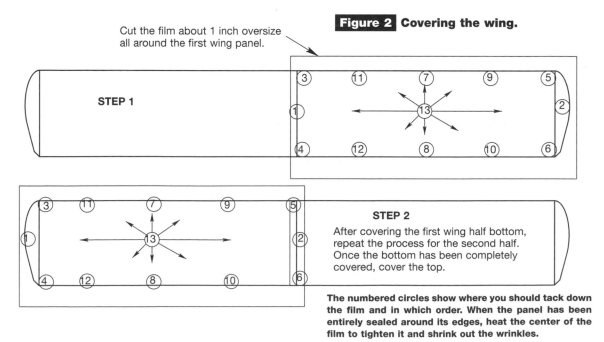

STEP 1

STEP 2

After covering the first wing half bottom, repeat the process for the second half. Once the bottom has been completely covered, cover the top.

The numbered circles show where you should tack down the film and in which order. When the panel has been entirely sealed around its edges, heat the center of the film to tighten it and shrink out the wrinkles.

Start covering the fuselage on the bottom. If the film can't be applied in one continuous piece, you'll have a seam; apply the aft film first, and work your way forward so that the seams "face" aft and will be less likely to be lifted by exhaust residue.

■ FUSELAGE. The four sides of the fuse-lage are the next largest sections to cover. To make the seams less obvious, cover the fuse bottom first, and then the left and right sides; cover the top last (see Figure 3). Also, if there will be seams in the film at the sides, start applying film at the tail and work toward the nose. By doing this, you ensure that the seam overlaps "face" backward, and that makes it less likely that exhaust residue will get under them.

As you did with the wing, start by tack-ing the front and back edges of the film down, and then move to the corners in a criss-cross pattern and continue until the entire perimeter is tacked down. Starting

kles out. After the tops have been covered, you can leave the wing as is, or you can run the iron gently over each of the ribs to bond the film to the cap-strips. This strengthens the wing. I tack the film down to every available wooden surface.

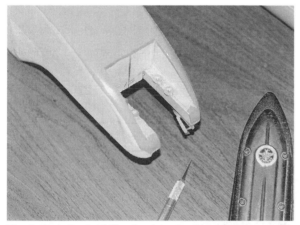

The bottom front of the fuselage has just been covered. Notice that the edges of the film go part way onto the side surfaces. Don't worry about the engine compartment yet; we'll address that area later.

Next, cover the tail parts. Notice that before I cover the flat surfaces, I cover the TEs with thin strips of film. This makes covering the edges much easier and minimizes wrinkles.

in the middle of one side, run the iron over the film, working your way out to the edges. Push trapped air out toward the edges, and poke really stubborn bubbles with a hobby knife or pin (to let the air escape) and then smooth the film flat. Trim the edges of the film so that it covers about ¼ inch of adjacent surfaces. By doing this, you ensure that when the other sides are covered, there will be a strong overlapping area between them; this will minimize the chance of the edges lifting later on.

Finally, cover the tail parts, fol-lowing the same procedures. Before I cover the sides of the control surfaces, I first cover all the edges with strips of ⅜-inch-

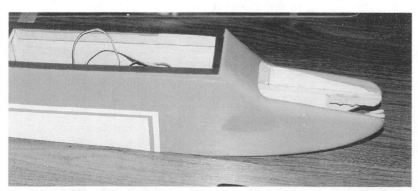

The sides and top of the fuselage have been covered. Again, pinstriping spiffs up our model's appearance.

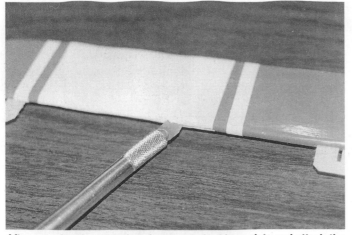

After covering the control surfaces, cut the hinge slots and attach the control surfaces to the model. By doing it this way, you'll be able to apply the trim and have it line up when you hinge and glue the surfaces into place.

with it as it flies high above.

Trim may be decals, self-adhesive trim material (available in sheets) or custom-cut pieces of the same type of iron-on covering film as you used to cover your model.

First make sure that the area to which the trim will be applied is absolutely clean—no dust. Mark where the trim is to be applied, and then, to minimize trapping air bubbles when you use iron-on material, remove the covering film from the center portion of this area; cut it away, leaving about a ¼-inch film "overlap" bond all around for the trim piece to bond to. Cut the trim to shape and apply it to the model. For a neat appearance, make sure all the edges are clean and straight.

If your kit doesn't have clear plastic win-

wide (approximately) film, centering them on the edges and ironing them down. Tack the film into place and work around the edges until you have completely sealed it down. Run the iron over the surfaces to remove all the wrinkles and shrink the film tightly down on them.

Well that's it. The film has been sealed down and is shrunk tight and wrinkle free. Hmmm … something's missing; the monotone finish could look prettier. Let's spiff it up some and add trim.

■ TRIM. There's nothing wrong with an all-white or an all-red model, but contrasting trim colors will add a lot to a model's appearance, and they'll enhance its visibility and help you to stay oriented

The windshield and window areas on this Nifty Fifty have been installed with chrome/silver trim for realism.

dows and windshields, use black, silver, or blue covering film to simulate them. Just make sure the color contrasts well with the model's overall finish. Black seems to be the standard color for numbers, but any contrasting color will do.

To decorate large areas in several colors, first remove the appropriate area of film along a straight line that is supported by a solid surface. The object is to avoid having many layers of film and to minimize the overlap of different pieces of film. If you want contrasting wingtips, remove the covering back to a rib and re-cover that part of

The covered model is looking good, but what about that engine compartment?

the wing with the new color.

Try to avoid covering open-bay wing areas with iron-on trim because it is very difficult to remove the wrinkles and bubbles that typically form. Finally, pinstriping tape (available at hobby shops) offers the chance to be creative and is easy to apply.

COLOR-SCHEME HINTS

For non-scale models, use colors that maximize your model's visibility because this will help you when you're learning to fly. Apply light colors to the top of the fuselage and wing and darker ones on the bottom. In the sunlight, everything has a shadow, and we tend to think of flying things as having shadows on the bottom. This will allow you to

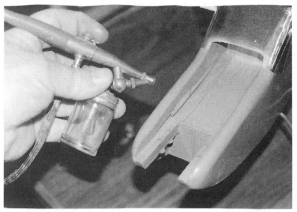

Paint the engine compartment with a fuelproof paint in a matching color (use an airbrush or a spray can).

Large or small, the attractive Nifty models aren't too difficult to finish with iron-on covering. Here, sharing its color scheme, a Nifty Fifty sits on top of a Giant Nifty. Both have been covered with translucent, colored, iron-on film.

tell—quickly and, eventually, automatically—whether your model is right side up or upside-down. Also, adding brightly contrasting colors to the wingtips and tail of a light-colored model makes it much easier to determine the model's attitude. Try to avoid monotonous color schemes, and avoid solid dark colors such as all black, blue, or silver. Black and blue tend to make a model blend into the background; silver and gray tend to reflect the color of the sky; a bright, light-colored model with contrasting trim is the easiest to see.

In the long run, a model's contrasting colors and finish can really affect how quickly you learn to fly it: they can make learning easy or difficult.

Field Equipment

The workshop is not the only place in which you'll need your tools; you'll need certain special equipment at the flying field to fuel, start and adjust your engine or prepare your electric model for flight. Tools and other equipment are best kept in toolboxes or specially designed field boxes, which can be simple or highly customized to suit your every need. At the field, I've seen everything from simple cardboard shoeboxes (not recommended) to custom-built, fold-out, bench-size maintenance stations. Your field box might evolve into a portable extension of your home workbench. Let's take a look at what you really need.

Figure 1 The field box.

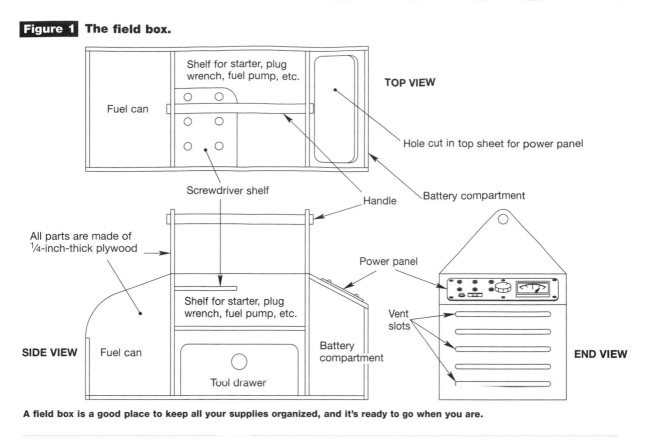

A field box is a good place to keep all your supplies organized, and it's ready to go when you are.

FIELD BOXES

Let's assume that you want a little more than a cardboard box to carry your tools to the flying field—great; there are plenty to choose from. Many companies offer fully assembled field boxes that are ready to go, but they also sell kits that allow you to build your own. Of course, you'll pay more for the ready-to-go boxes; the kit boxes are usually made of plywood parts that have been cut to shape and just have to be glued together. If you've built a model airplane, assembling a field-box kit will be a piece of cake. Use any glue you like: CA, aliphatic resin or epoxy; it doesn't make much difference. But you *must* make the box fuelproof. A finishing coat of polyurethane will make the box look better and last longer, and it will be easier to clean it after a day at the field.

If you decide to design and build a field box, lauan plywood is an excellent choice of material and is available at most home-improvement centers. Use Figure 1 as a guide. Remember, you want to carry only what you know you'll need—the basics—not every tool in your workshop. A relatively compact box with one or two small drawers and a shelf at the top is ideal; and a strong dowel handle will make it easy to carry.

Some field boxes have supports that will hold your model as you work on it; depending on the

size of your model, this is a good feature, but a separate stand is sometimes more convenient to use. Again, you can buy a stand or make one yourself.

As your involvement in the hobby grows, the number of tools you consider "basic" may increase. In the beginning, a simple screwdriver and wrench may satisfy your basic maintenance requirements, but you might eventually want a more complete set

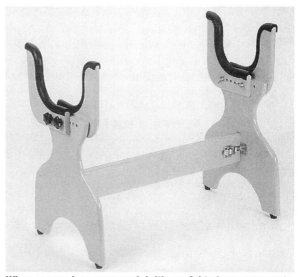

When you work on your model, it's useful to have a separate stand for it. This one folds for storage and has padded support arms.

of tools for field use; a separate field toolbox is the answer.

The goal is to have a neat way of taking your tools to the flying field. After very many years of modeling, I guess I've gone overboard: I have a field box for basic supplies and several other boxes containing equipment that suits the type of flying I

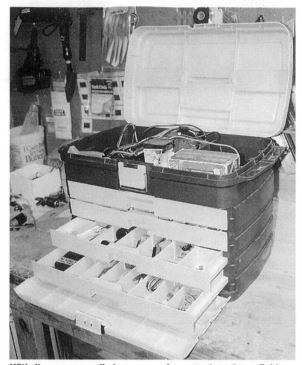

With its many small drawers and compartments, a fishing-tackle box also makes a good flying-field tools organizer. It makes finding your tools easy.

intend to do on a particular day: one for glow-powered models; another for gasoline-powered, giant-scale models; yet another, smaller, box for electric-powered models. But for now, let's talk about that first model's requirements.

To get our engine-powered model airborne, we need to bring the engine to life: we need fuel, a spark and air. Air is a readily available "freebie," so I'll address the fuel and spark.

PUMPING FUEL

We need a way to get the fuel out of the jug and into the fuel tank—some sort of pump to put the fuel into the tank and remove what's left at the end of the day.

■ **FUEL BULB**—the least expensive option. It's nothing more than a rubber bulb attached to a length of fuel tubing; the bulb works just like a turkey baster on Thanksgiving. To draw fuel from your jug, simply insert the fuel tubing and squeeze the bulb. As the bulb inflates, it draws fuel into the

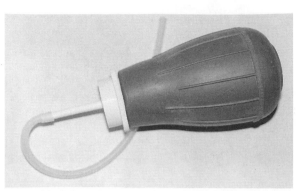

The fuel bulb is perhaps the oldest way to get fuel into your model's tank; it's certainly the least expensive way.

tubing; then attach the tubing to your tank's outlet tube (with a small section of brass tubing), and squeeze the bulb to fill the tank. You'll have to do this several times to completely fill the tank, but there is no cheaper way of getting the juice into your model.

Du-Bro offers a special fuel jug that comes with a two-way bulb attached to its cap with a length of tubing. It's a popular fueling system that's worth looking at. Small balls in the bulb act as check valves and prevent fuel from backing up. This system is available in both glow-fuel and gasoline versions.

■ **MECHANICAL PUMP**—a quicker way to fuel your model. It has a crank handle: simply crank it in one direction to fuel and in the other direction to defuel. A mechanical pump has an outer case and nipples to which you hook the fuel tubing; some are geared to speed fuel transfer (fewer turns of the handle are needed). Whichever type of mechanical pump you use, attach a fuel-line filter to the inlet tube to lengthen its life by keeping debris out.

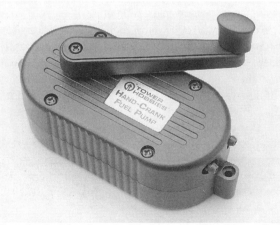

A mechanical, hand-cranked fuel pump such as this one from Tower Hobbies transfers fuel more quickly than a fuel bulb can.

This mechanical fuel pump has rollers that squeeze the tubing to pump the fuel. It has few moving parts, so it lasts a long time.

A good 12V electric starter is a wise investment. Its powerful motor produces enough torque to turn your engine over, and the rubber starter cone prevents the starter from slipping.

During many years of use, my electric fuel pump never caused me any problems. It transfers about 12 ounces of fuel in about 1 minute. (Note the fuel filter at the end of the fuel tubing.)

■ ELECTRIC FUEL PUMP—yet another choice; requiring no effort to use, it's very popular indeed. Again, there are several brands.

STARTING THE ENGINE

After fueling our model, we need to turn the engine over. You could use your fingers to flip that propeller, but I can't recommend it! (One backfire will show you how painful that sharp blade can be.)

■ "CHICKEN STICK" (starter stick)—use one that has a padded surface that won't damage the prop when you flip it over. You can buy such a stick or make one with a length of ½-inch-diameter dowel covered with electrical tape or a section of

automotive rubber hose. The finger you save may be your own.

■ ELECTRIC STARTER—offers by far the safest and easiest way to turn your engine over, but understandably, it's more expensive than a stick. Most of the many available standard starters require a 12V battery and come with a 2- or 3-foot electrical cord so they are easy to move into position. They have large alligator battery clips to attach the cord to the battery terminals. Electric starters may also be powered by rechargeable Ni-Cds or by a power panel that can service several other electrical devices.

BATTERIES AND POWER PANELS

■ STARTER BATTERY—can be a small motorcycle battery or a maintenance-free gel-cell; in fact, most commercial field boxes are designed to incorporate a battery and a power panel to operate your starter, electric fuel pump and the glow-driver power cord that's used to ignite the engine's glow plug (again, see Figure 1). Two power cords exit the rear of the panel and are attached to your 12V battery.

■ POWER PANEL—the ends of your starter and fuel-pump power cords require special plug-in clips so they can easily be plugged into the power panel. The clips usually come with the panel. The power panel has an amp meter (ammeter) and an adjustment knob so you can check and adjust the strength of your glow driver (see next page). The

To save your fingers when starting your engine, use a padded "chicken stick" to flip the prop; the padding protects your prop blade.

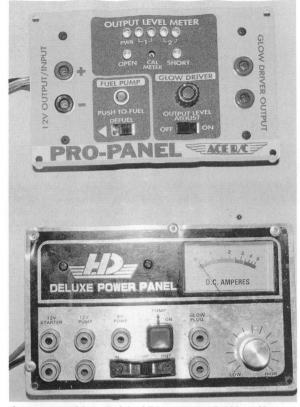

A power panel is a useful addition to your field box. You can run a starter, a fuel pump and a glow-plug driver with either of these: the Ace Pro-Panel (top) uses a series of LEDs in place of the ammeter used on the panel shown.

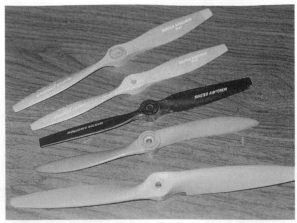

There are thousands of props to choose from—plastic and wood and in several styles. Use the size recommended by your engine's manufacturer.

meter also indicates whether the glow-plug element is good or not and can tell whether your engine is flooded by showing how much current is flowing to the element.

■ **GLOW DRIVER**—available separately from the power panel, it also needs plug-in clips attached to the end of its cord. The glow-driver cord is not the only way to energize your glow plug; you may also use a Ni-Cd-powered glow driver such as the Du-Bro Kwik-Start, which is a 1.2V cell attached to a tube clip that you attach to the top of the glow plug.

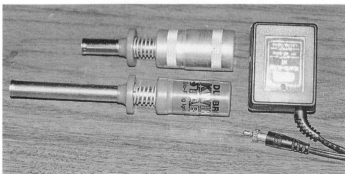

Ni-Cd-powered glow drivers like these useful, Du-Bro, clip-on Kwik-Starts are convenient to use. If you need to, you can replace the Ni-Cd cell by unscrewing the top of the glow driver's case.

Simply attach it to your glow plug, and you're ready to go. McDaniel R/C also offers Ni-Cd-powered glow drivers—Ni-Starters. Like the Kwik-Start, this comes with its own charger and is available with an ammeter attached to it. This meter works in the same way as the power-panel meter, but it's much smaller.

■ **GLOW-PLUG WRENCH**—a basic requirement for installing and removing glow plugs. It's worth having two, so you'll always have one in your field box.

PROPELLERS
The ongoing argument is whether wooden or plastic props are better; the answer is that it all depends on your requirements. Whichever type you choose, use the size of prop suggested by your engine's manufacturer,

A glow-plug wrench is a basic requirement. This one from Du-Bro has three tapped openings to hold additional glow plugs.

or follow the recommendations of fellow modelers who use the same engine (see also Chapter 13, "Prop Talk").

■ **WOODEN PROP**—generally less expensive, so in the beginning, you might want to use wood; it will break easily if it hits the ground and will thus absorb the impact forces instead of transmitting them to your engine.

■ **PLASTIC PROP** (sometimes, fiber-filled resin)—does not break as easily and therefore lasts longer. Many of the newer ones, such as APC props by Landing Products, are more efficient than inexpensive wooden props: in many applications, they offer greater performance for a given horsepower.

You must balance your prop blades: remove material from the tip of the heavier blade until the two blades balance. A balanced prop vibrates less than one that's out of balance.

PROP BALANCING

Before using it, you should always balance your prop; a balanced prop produces much less vibration than one that isn't balanced. A prop balancer isn't really field equipment; I recommend that you buy one or make your own (see Figure 2).

For more information on selecting a prop of the right size and on prop balancing, see Chapter 13, "Prop Talk."

■ **PROP REAMER**—removes material evenly because its cutting surfaces are on the sides instead of in the front as on a drill bit (see Figure 3). The steps on the reamer help keep the hole perpendicular to the face of the prop. Reamers are available in

If the hole in the prop is too small for the engine's prop shaft, enlarge it with a prop reamer—not a regular drill bit, as this may elongate the hole.

metric and standard U.S. sizes, so use the right one for your engine (check at your hobby shop).

ALSO USEFUL ...

■ **SPINNER**—worth considering, especially if you use an electric starter. It allows an electric starter to

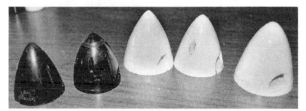

A spinner will improve your model's looks and make it easier to attach the electric starter. The openings in the side of the spinner should not touch the prop blades; if they do, enlarge them with a hobby knife.

Figure 2 **Homemade prop balancer.**

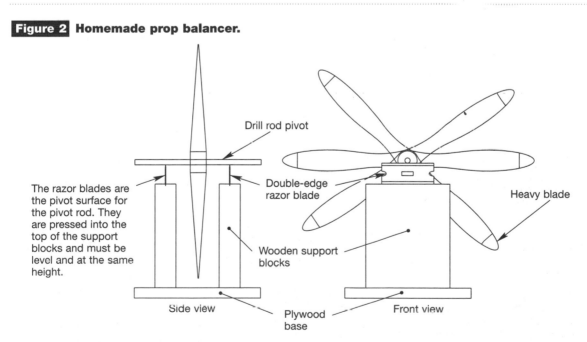

Drill rod pivot

The razor blades are the pivot surface for the pivot rod. They are pressed into the top of the support blocks and must be level and at the same height.

Double-edge razor blade

Wooden support blocks

Side view

Plywood base

Heavy blade

Front view

To balance the prop blades, remove material from the heavier blade's tip until, after being spun, the prop consistently stops at random positions.

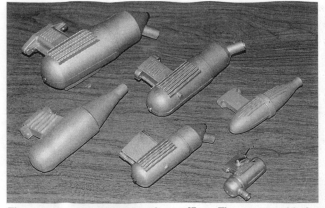

There are several standard engine mufflers. These come with the engine and should always be used; less engine noise and better performance are the goals.

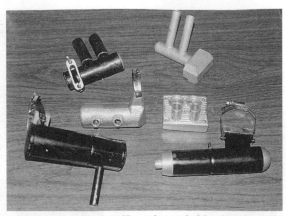

If you need a special muffler ask your hobby shop for help; they're available separately (as "aftermarket" add-ons), but they aren't all equally effective. Some are designed to be concealed inside the engine cowl.

be attached firmly to the engine, and it helps to prevent the rubber starter cone from slipping off when you start the engine. A spinner also really dresses up your model's looks, and because it streamlines it, it helps to reduce drag.

Available in plastic and metal, all spinners have a backplate that fits between the prop and the engine's thrust washer. The spinner cone either snaps into place on the backplate or must be attached with screws. Special openings in the spinner should allow the prop blades to pass through without touching the spinner. In plastic spinners, if the openings are too small, you can usually enlarge them with your hobby knife.

■ 12V DC FIELD BATTERY CHARGER—very nice to have, as it allows you to quickly top off your battery cells at the field. Make sure your field charger has the correct output voltage to properly charge your battery pack. Some have dual output voltage so they can charge both the TX and RX packs.

■ EXPANDED-SCALE VOLTMETER (ESV)—to check the voltage of your flight-pack battery. To safely determine how much flight time you have, you should check the voltage of your RX battery. If you have a 4-cell pack, do not fly with less than 4.8 volts. For a quick check, there are also battery condition meters that simply have green and red fields.

Figure 3 Reaming the prop hole.

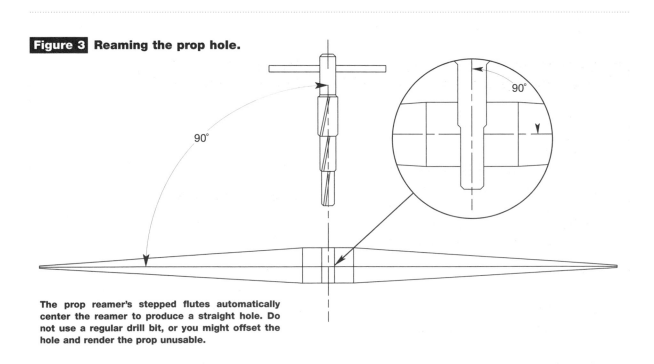

90°

90°

The prop reamer's stepped flutes automatically center the reamer to produce a straight hole. Do not use a regular drill bit, or you might offset the hole and render the prop unusable.

Most experienced modelers have such a meter, and you'll need one, too.

NOISE SUPPRESSION

As well as being good for consistent engine performance, a muffler is often required by clubs officially recognized by the Academy of Model Aeronautics (AMA). A muffler suppresses engine noise and supplies backpressure to help the power cycle. Many engines come with a muffler so it doesn't cost you any extra to be quieter.

If your engine doesn't come with a muffler, there are many available "aftermarket" mufflers, and some fit inside the engine cowl for an improved scale look. Others drastically reduce engine noise.

Most standard mufflers have an attached pressure fitting (nipple) that supplies muffler pressure to the fuel tank and ensures consistent fuel delivery to the carb.

Some mufflers have baffles while others simply act as exhaust deflectors and have only a minor muffling effect. Whichever muffler you choose, have someone from the local club check your engine's noise level with a decibel (dB) meter; it should be less than 99dB.

CREATURE COMFORTS

Finally, let's look at items that make it easier to work on your model.
• A stand or small folding card table—gets your model off the ground so makes it a lot easier on your back.
• A mat, piece of carpet or a towel to put your model on. If you drop a small part or screw, it will be a lot

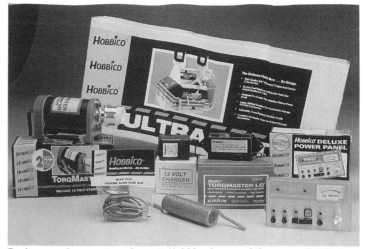

Basic ground-support equipment: Hobbico is one of the many distributors that offers special, money-saving, field-equipment package deals. Look for them at the hobby shop.

easier to find than if it fell into the grass!
• A cooler containing something to eat and drink. If you plan to spend most of the day at the field, or if you are traveling out of town to an event, snacks and drinks will keep you going.
• A folding lawn chair so you have somewhere to sit.
• A sun umbrella or pole tent.

Get together with others who plan to fly at the same time, and have everyone take along something to make a picnic. You get the idea: if you want to have fun, make sure you're comfortable.

Traveling a long way to fly and then discovering that you left your field box, fuel or even your radio at home is very frustrating. Develop a checklist, and look it over before you go to the flying field. Plan to have fun! You did bring the wing didn't you?

Before you leave for a day at the flying field, check:

MODEL
❑ Wing
❑ Fuselage
❑ Wing hold-down bolts or rubber bands
❑ Engine; is the needle valve in the carburetor?
❑ Transmitter; is the battery fully charged?
❑ Is the radio operating correctly, and do the controls move in the proper directions?

SUPPLIES
❑ Fuel
❑ Fuel pump
❑ Extra glow plugs and glow-plug wrench

❑ Spare propeller
❑ Prop wrench
❑ Paper towels and spray cleaner (degreaser, 409 etc.)

CREATURE COMFORTS
❑ Cooler containing snacks and soda/ice water
❑ Folding lawn chair
❑ Sunscreen
❑ Sunglasses
❑ Large-brim hat
❑ Trash bag to keep field clean

Learning to Fly

Well, here we are; we've built our model, broken in the engine and become familiar with its operation. The engine has a reliable idle, our radio batteries are fully charged, and the weather outside is beautiful. There's a light breeze blowing down the runway, so there's nothing left to do but fly. Great! Let's start with ground school.

You and your instructor should develop a training plan. For every flight session, you should have a goal and should build on what you've already learned. Only after you have mastered the tasks at hand should you go on to the next.

A good way to start is to learn how to taxi, then take off, fly straight and level, turn left and right, and fly at low airspeeds. You will learn how to stall your model and recover from a stall, how to fly at lower altitudes and then to set up for your first landing approach. At all times, concentrate on keeping your model under control and adjusting for wind conditions. Let's give it a try.

Figure 1 Engine torque.

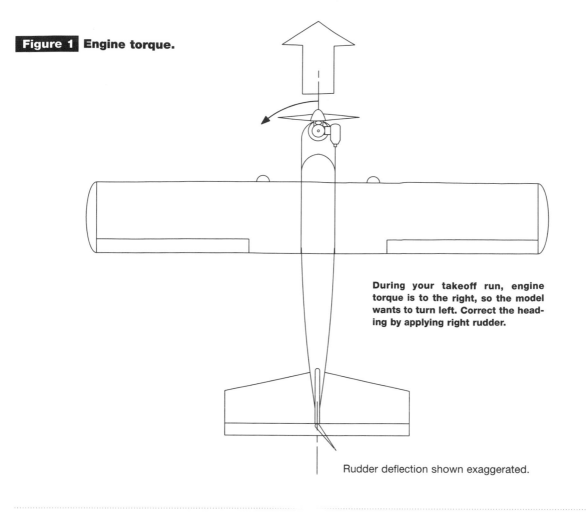

During your takeoff run, engine torque is to the right, so the model wants to turn left. Correct the heading by applying right rudder.

Rudder deflection shown exaggerated.

THE BUDDY SYSTEM

Many student pilots train by using a buddy box. This system has a cable that connects the student's and the instructor's radios and allows the instructor to switch the student's radio controls on and off; for the system to work, the radios must be compatible. (Information on this system is available from all radio manufacturers.)

First, the student sets up his radio and model, and then the two radios are connected by a trainer cable. Next, both radios' trim levers are adjusted so they are the same; this is so that the model's trim will not change when the trainer switch is thrown.

In practice, using his radio, the instructor takes off and flies the student's model to a safe altitude. When the model is flying straight and level, the instructor simply activates the trainer switch and holds it in the "on" position. Then control is transferred to the student's radio, and the student flies the model. If the student gets into trouble, the instructor can simply release the spring-loaded switch and regain control of the aircraft.

Compared with using just one radio that has to be handed back and forth between the student and the instructor, the buddy-box system is much easier on the model, *and* it helps the student to relax and concentrate. Many clubs consider it the preferred training system.

TAXI TESTS

After going through your *preflight checklist* (see Appendix 5 on page 120 at the end of the book), start the engine and check its settings, then slowly taxi the model up and down the runway. Your instructor should let you get the feel of the model on the ground before you actually fly it. Notice that when you taxi *with* the wind, the rudder is slightly less effective than when you taxi *into* it.

If you are about to fly a tail-dragger, apply a little up-elevator to keep the tailwheel planted firmly on the ground. Conversely, if you're piloting a tricycle-gear model, for maximum steering control, you need to apply a little down-elevator to firmly hold the nose wheel down. Taxiing is also a way to learn "reverse steering": when the model is pointing toward you, left and right are reversed! At first, this can be very confusing, but with practice, you'll learn to automatically adjust your control actions when the model turns toward you.

Practice advancing the throttle slowly to minimize the effects of engine torque. As you advance the throttle, notice that the model tends to swerve to the left. Correct this by applying a little right rudder as the throttle is advanced (see Figure 1). Keep a light touch on the controls, as a heavy-handed approach will lead to over-controlling the model, and this can make it swerve around.

Once you're comfortable with taxiing and can guide your model anywhere you want without losing control, you're ready for the next exciting step: takeoff!

TAKEOFF

For the most part, your model's first few flights will be fully controlled by your instructor; he will both take off and land it (see Figure 2, which shows the takeoff and landing sequence). As you learn to anticipate your model's movements and show the required control, your instructor will at last tell you, "Go ahead; take it off this time!" (By the way, always try to take off into the wind—not downwind!)

You'll find that taking off is actually quite easy. Most trainers are stable and will climb all by themselves when you advance the throttle. You'll have to concentrate on maintaining heading and pitch control, though.

Slowly advance the throttle and correct the model's heading with rudder (add a little right rudder to keep it going straight down the runway). Listen to the engine, and make sure that it is putting out full power.

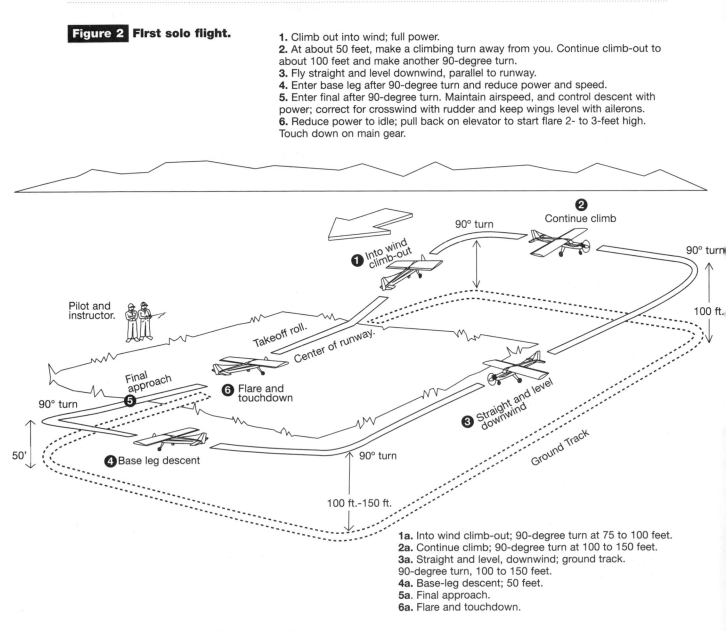

Figure 2 **First solo flight.**

1. Climb out into wind; full power.
2. At about 50 feet, make a climbing turn away from you. Continue climb-out to about 100 feet and make another 90-degree turn.
3. Fly straight and level downwind, parallel to runway.
4. Enter base leg after 90-degree turn and reduce power and speed.
5. Enter final after 90-degree turn. Maintain airspeed, and control descent with power; correct for crosswind with rudder and keep wings level with ailerons.
6. Reduce power to idle; pull back on elevator to start flare 2- to 3-feet high. Touch down on main gear.

1a. Into wind climb-out; 90-degree turn at 75 to 100 feet.
2a. Continue climb; 90-degree turn at 100 to 150 feet.
3a. Straight and level, downwind; ground track. 90-degree turn, 100 to 150 feet.
4a. Base-leg descent; 50 feet.
5a. Final approach.
6a. Flare and touchdown.

The instructor's radio has a trainer switch. By holding the switch on, the instructor activates the student's controls. If the student pilot loses control, the instructor simply releases the switch to gain control of the model.

As the model gets light on the wheels, pull back slightly on the elevator stick, and let its nose rise slightly. Keep the wings level with the ailerons, and let the model climb out at a 20- to 25-degree angle relative to the ground. If the model jumps off the ground and heads upward at a steeper angle, don't panic; ease off the elevator stick and, if necessary, apply a little down-elevator; push the elevator stick forward slightly to keep the model at the proper angle of attack.

Note that even during the climb-out, you may have to keep applying a little right rudder so the model will stay straight on course. This is partly because of engine torque on the ground and P-factor (asymmetrical thrust) from the prop during the climb-out. Once the model is at a safe altitude (100 to 150 feet), it's time to turn it around.

BANKING AND TURNING

After takeoff, you must learn how to turn the model left and right. Without knowing this basic maneuver, we'd all lose a lot of models over the horizon. As mentioned earlier, ailerons make a model roll, and this is the first step in making a turn. First apply left or right aileron and bank the model over 15 to 20 degrees from level; then add up-elevator to bring the model around and begin the turn. To increase or decrease the radius of the turn, add more or less elevator; aileron input remains about the same. As you add the aileron and elevator inputs, you must also increase the throttle slightly to make up for the added drag that will slow the model down and make it descend.

When the model is on the heading you want, release up-elevator and apply a little opposite aileron to bring the wings back to level. Finally, bring the throttle back to the previous power setting for straight and level flight. Now you're flying

in a new direction. Wow!

If you fly your model straight away from yourself, a 180-degree turn will bring it back to you. Remember: on the return leg, *your* left is not the model's left; they're opposite! When the model is flying away from you, moving the aileron stick to the left will make its left wing drop. When it's coming toward you, its left wing is on your right. The sooner you can react to this situation, the sooner you will become a proficient R/C pilot.

A simple way to guide your model when it flies toward you is to move the aileron stick in the direction of the lower wing panel. Look at the oncoming model; if the wing on the right side is low, moving the stick to your right will lift that wing and return the model to straight and level. Think of it as using the aileron stick to prop up that lowered wing panel. This technique works really well and goes a long way toward eliminating confusion when the model is flying toward you (see Figure 3).

Figure 3 **Leveling the wings.**

When the model is flying toward you, left and right commands will feel reversed. Move the aileron stick toward the lower wing to raise it.

For most students, the most difficult thing to learn is how to react correctly to the model's attitude when it is very far away and looks like a dark silhouette. In this situation, pay close attention to its flight path.

It is important to become comfortable with all maneuvers. You should be able to turn left and right accurately (both coming and going) and to maintain a constant altitude during your turns before you move to the next step: landing.

Figure 4 When the wing stalls.

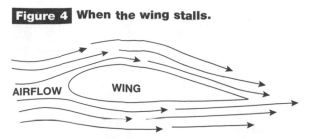

1. In normal flight, the airflow over and under the wing is smooth and undisturbed.

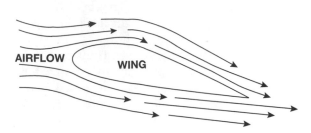

2. As the wing's angle of attack (AoA) increases, the airflow is initially uniform above and below the wing.

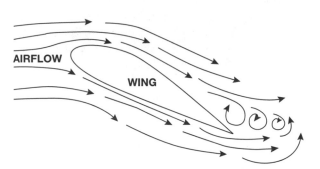

3. The higher the AoA angle, the harder it is for the airflow to stay attached to the airfoil shape of the wing. The airflow starts to separate at the trailing edge.

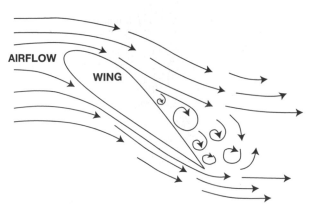

4. At a critical AoA, the airflow over the wing completely separates, and the wing stalls. It stops flying

LANDING

Takeoffs are optional; landings are absolutely required. How well our model comes back to the ground determines its longevity. But there is only one way to become good at landings—practice!

We start landing practice at a safe altitude by first learning how to fly at a low throttle setting. We must trim our model to fly slowly without losing altitude. If we don't slow our model down, we'll never make a successful landing. As you bring the throttle back, you must pull the model's nose up slightly to prevent it from descending. This higher angle of attack (AoA) slows the model's airspeed. Up-elevator increases the model's AoA; down-elevator decreases its AoA. A greater AoA slows the model, and a lower AoA increases airspeed.

The model's descent is primarily controlled with throttle. We want to land our model at or slightly above the model's stall speed, so we must first learn what that speed is and then practice flying the model into and out of the stalled condition. You can stall the model by pulling back on the elevator stick so that the AoA increases and speed decreases until the model stops flying. It will fall forward, or one of the wings will drop. Experiment, and you'll learn how to recover. Once we know where and when the model will stall (in the air), we can land on the ground (see Figure 4: stall sequence).

SETTING UP FOR LANDING

There are four basic parts of the landing pattern:
• downwind leg;
• base leg;
• final approach;
• flare.

We always want to land with the nose into the wind to keep the model's airspeed as high as possible while minimizing its ground speed. The two turns from downwind to base and from base to final should be 90-degree turns and should be done with 15 to 20 degrees of bank (see Figure 2). The only difference between these turns and those we have already learned is that throttle is reduced to allow the model to descend.

With the model traveling on its downwind leg (at the far side of the runway and directly in front of you), pull the throttle back to about half, and pull back on the elevator stick a little to slow the model down. As it descends to about 50 feet of altitude, turn 90 degrees to the base leg and then straighten the wing back to level.

Remember to control the descent with throttle and airspeed with elevator (pitch) control. Don't

Just before touching down, feed in more up-elevator (note elevator deflection), and flare to bleed off excess airspeed. Once you're down, stay on the rudder and let the model run out straight down the runway.

stall the model by pulling all the way back on elevator, but fly just above the stall speed.

Turn 90 degrees again to begin the final approach, and set up the model by lining it up with the runway centerline. We're looking for a descent angle that will bring the model in contact with the runway just as we slow it to stall speed. The flare (pulling the nose up gradually just before the model contacts the ground) eliminates excess speed and prevents the model from bouncing back into the air.

Once you've flared and the model has touched down nicely on the runway, just keep on the rudder and let the model roll out straight ahead until it comes to rest. Phew! That wasn't too hard, was it?!

Nothing else gives you such a feeling of satisfaction as that first perfect landing. You'll spend the rest of your hobby career perfecting your landing skills. Crosswinds and gusty days always challenge you to improve. This is where "touch-and-go's" come in handy (a maneuver in which you touch the wheels to the ground as if to land and immediately power up and resume flight). Just remember to always keep ahead of the model mentally; know what you're going to do next so the model does not

get ahead of you. Plan your flight and fly your plan. Stay in control.

So, there you are; you've gone to the flying field, you've "committed aviation," and you've made that first great landing without anything breaking or falling off your model. Congratulations; you're in! Now all you have to do is have fun and practice. The rest is all gravy.

HAND-LAUNCHING

Another way to get your model into the air is to hand-launch it. This works well for models with small wheels and at flying fields with long grass; and it's the only way to launch electric gliders, which have no landing gear. A certain amount of care is required, though, as you are handling a model on which the propeller is spinning.

To successfully launch a model by hand, you must hold it firmly just behind its center of gravity with one hand while you support its nose with the other hand. Hold the model overhead with its nose and wings level; then, after taking a few quick steps, throw it, javelin style. Don't launch it in a steep, climbing attitude, as this quickly slows it down and often leads to a stall and crash shortly after release.

The proper technique is to launch the model level or pointed at or just above the horizon. The launcher must be careful to avoid being struck by the tail, and he should always keep his hands clear of the propeller.

Models without landing gear usually land with the engine turned off; the model simply touches down and slides in on its belly. Almost all electric-powered gliders use this method.

Hand-launching also allows you to fly out of areas from which landing-gear-equipped models can't be flown.

When you hand-launch a model, hold it just behind its CG, take a few quick steps, then throw it at or just above the horizon, javelin-style.

Try to release the model with the wings level. Don't pitch it upward; it might stall.

11

Basic Maneuvers and Aerobatics

You've learned the basics of taking off and landing, and thanks to your instructor, you did so without doing too much damage to your model. You can now go to the field whenever you want to and fly at will—yea! Being an R/C pilot is a journey as well as a goal; taking off and landing is only the beginning. It's what happens in between that makes flying so much fun.

Figure 1 Headwind, crosswind and tailwind.

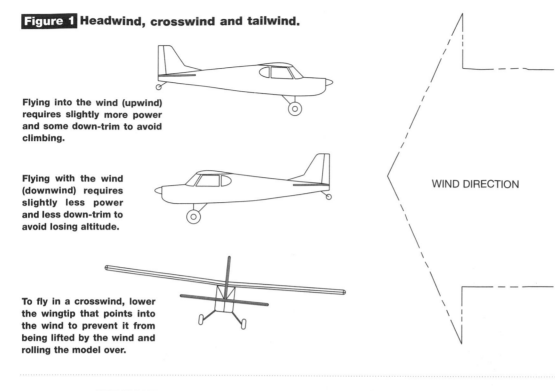

Flying into the wind (upwind) requires slightly more power and some down-trim to avoid climbing.

Flying with the wind (downwind) requires slightly less power and less down-trim to avoid losing altitude.

To fly in a crosswind, lower the wingtip that points into the wind to prevent it from being lifted by the wind and rolling the model over.

WIND DIRECTION

STRAIGHT AND LEVEL

Flying straight and level requires a little more than just keeping the model's wings level and its nose pointed straight ahead. Flying is a three-dimensional experience; we must be aware of the need to make minor pitch, roll and yaw corrections. Flying on calm, windless days is great, but such perfect conditions are rare. What's the biggest challenge? Wind—especially crosswind.

Our reference is always the runway centerline, and to fly, say, 50 feet above it on a parallel course requires us to compensate for the effects of wind. Flying straight into the wind (headwind) requires certain power and elevator trim settings to maintain a constant altitude. If you fly *with* the wind (downwind), the required power and trim settings will be different. The effect of flying downwind instead of upwind, although very slight, is that ground speed changes. When flying downwind, your model's ground speed is equal to its airspeed plus wind speed. When flying upwind, i.e., into a headwind, its ground speed equals its airspeed minus the wind speed. Going downwind, the throttle can be backed off slightly, and heading into the wind, slightly more power is required (see Figure 1).

What about flying in a slight crosswind? To track straight over the runway centerline, we have to "crab" the model slightly sideways with its nose pointed slightly into the wind (see Figure 2). The strength of the crosswind will affect how much

Figure 2 Crab angle for crosswind.

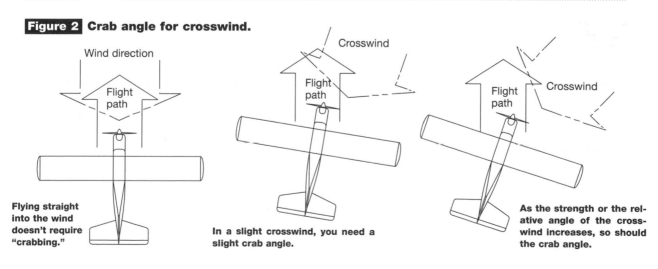

Wind direction

Flight path

Flying straight into the wind doesn't require "crabbing."

Crosswind

Flight path

In a slight crosswind, you need a slight crab angle.

Crosswind

Flight path

As the strength or the relative angle of the crosswind increases, so should the crab angle.

Figure 3 **First roll.**

To start, use only aileron and elevator and about three-quarters throttle.

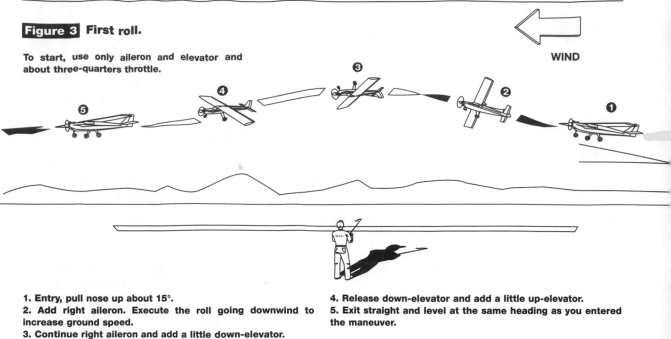

WIND

1. Entry, pull nose up about 15°.
2. Add right aileron. Execute the roll going downwind to increase ground speed.
3. Continue right aileron and add a little down-elevator.

4. Release down-elevator and add a little up-elevator.
5. Exit straight and level at the same heading as you entered the maneuver.

crab angle is required to keep our flight path straight and parallel with the runway. Think of this crosswind/crab-angle relationship as similar to rowing a boat across a river. If you want to go straight across, you have to row against the current at a certain angle. The use of rudder and aileron is very important here. In a very strong crosswind, the wingtip that points into the wind should be kept down slightly to prevent it from catching the wind, being lifted and rolling the model over.

Wind gusts (turbulence) also do their best to disturb a model's flight path. For the most part, however, slight deviations from true straight and level can be overlooked—until you're setting up for more advanced maneuvers.

Flying a 90-degree turn without losing or gaining airspeed and without changing altitude is an initial goal. With practice, you'll notice slight changes in pitch and airspeed as wind conditions change, and you'll be able to react to correct them. Eventually, your turns in either direction—regardless of wind conditions—will be precise and smooth. This skill is particularly important when you set up your landing approach.

AEROBATICS

For the most part, I'll discuss sport aerobatics—not competition-level maneuvers. Anyone can loop or roll a trainer fairly easily. But doing these maneuvers precisely and exactly where you want them takes practice.

Start maneuvers at 200 to 300 feet in altitude (two or three mistakes high!), and as you gain confidence in your ability, bring the maneuvers down

Figure 4 **Roll without elevator compensation.**

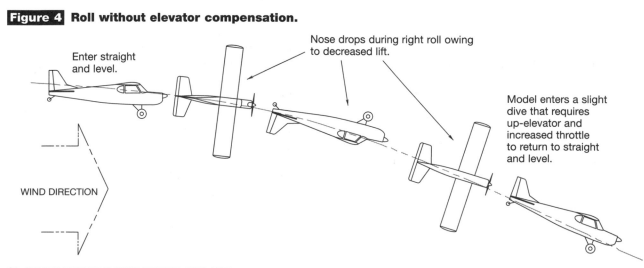

Enter straight and level.

Nose drops during right roll owing to decreased lift.

Model enters a slight dive that requires up-elevator and increased throttle to return to straight and level.

WIND DIRECTION

Figure 5 Loop entry.

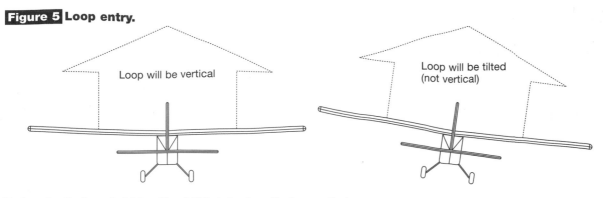

Loop will be vertical

Loop will be tilted (not vertical)

Try to enter the loop straight and level. This helps keep the loop vertical.

to 50 or 75 feet. Try to imagine a straight line in front of you, and try to fly the model exactly along it. Regardless of the wind, you should be able to fly this line precisely and in both directions.

In all aerobatic maneuvers, throttle management is important. Use as much power as you need to climb, and then throttle back on the way down.

ROLLS AND LOOPS

Looping and rolling are involved in every type of aerobatic maneuver. At first, banging the controls hard over makes you think these two maneuvers are as easy as pie. It isn't until you start to demand more precision from yourself that you find it just isn't so.

■ **HORIZONTAL ROLLS** aren't that difficult when done at a high roll rate, but when done more slowly (say, 2 or 3 seconds per rotation), the demands on rudder and elevator are increased.

To roll:
• To do a simple roll (see Figure 3), the model must start at a slightly nose-high attitude. It's a good idea to point the nose slightly downward, accelerate for a while and then raise the nose to begin the maneuver—bringing a "reserve" of energy into the roll. This is because as you roll the model, its nose begins to drop because of the reduction of lift (see Figure 4). If started straight and level with the elevator at neutral, a roll will end up in a slight dive. Start the roll on a slightly ascending flight path.
• Flying downwind, from straight and level, bring the nose up slightly and add right aileron.
• While constantly holding right aileron and neutral elevator, add a little left rudder to hold the nose up as your model adopts an attitude with the wingtips pointing straight up and down (known as "knife-edge").
• As you roll past knife-edge, start to reduce left rudder and to add down-elevator.

• As you enter inverted flight, down-elevator should be holding the nose up, and there shouldn't be any left rudder.
• As you break out of inverted, reduce down-elevator slightly and slowly apply a little right rudder to keep the nose up.
• As you enter the roll's second knife-edge, the elevator should again be at neutral, and right rudder should be holding the nose up.
• Finally, as the model continues its roll to straight and level, rudder input should be released.

Phew! Whoever said a roll was so simple?

When you've gained confidence and can roll both left and right, you can start to level the maneuver and slow the roll rate.

■ **LOOPS** require that, while keeping the model on a constant heading, you simultaneously manage elevator, rudder, ailerons and throttle to make the loop as round as possible. The larger the loop's diameter, the more time it will take to complete and the more corrections you'll have to make to keep it on track. A loop you can complete comfortably in about 3 or 4 seconds is a reasonable size to aim for.

To loop:
• Start by flying absolutely straight and level upwind; if you don't, your loop will become a corkscrew kind of thing (see Figure 5).
• As you pull up from straight and level, use a little right rudder to cope with engine torque as you raise the nose (see Figure 6).
• As the model flies up the vertical leg of the loop and starts to go inverted, keep the wings level with aileron and ease off slightly on the elevator.
• Coming down the back half of the loop, the model will gain speed considerably, so you must pull the throttle back. Adjust elevator as required to keep the loop round.
• At the bottom of the loop, as you exit the maneu-

Figure 6 Loop.

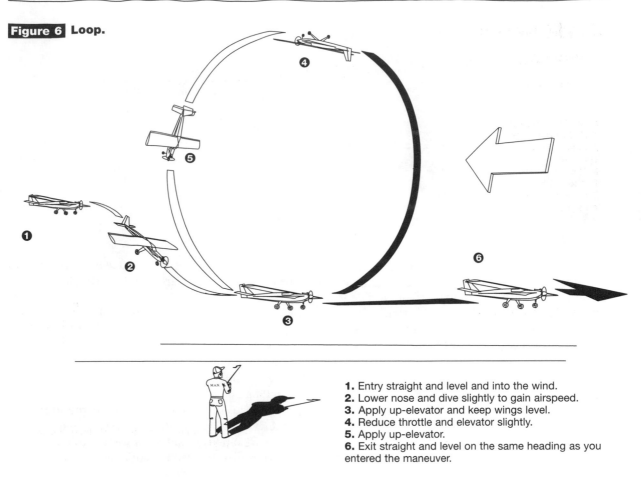

1. Entry straight and level and into the wind.
2. Lower nose and dive slightly to gain airspeed.
3. Apply up-elevator and keep wings level.
4. Reduce throttle and elevator slightly.
5. Apply up-elevator.
6. Exit straight and level on the same heading as you entered the maneuver.

ver and return to straight and level, your model should be at the same altitude and heading as it started at.

Combining loops and rolls allows you to complete more advanced maneuvers.

■ **IMMELEMANN TURN**—a half loop topped off with a half roll; the model exits the maneuver at a higher altitude than it started at and is heading in the opposite direction (see Figure 7).

■ **SPLIT-S**—the opposite of an Immelemann turn. Start at a high altitude with a half roll to inverted, and follow with a half loop. The model loses altitude and ends up straight and level and heading in the opposite direction (see Figure 8).

■ **SUSTAINED INVERTED FLIGHT**—requires either a half loop or a half roll to the inverted position. Then use a little down-elevator to prevent the nose from dropping. The same half loop or roll brings the model back into straight and level flight.

■ **HAMMERHEAD STALL**—entering and exiting

this or a wingover requires a quarter loop.

■ **SQUARE LOOP**—has four quarter loops (one in each corner) and inverted flight at the top.

SPINS AND SNAP ROLLS

Spins and snap rolls ("snaps") are similar in that both require that you stall the model before starting the maneuver.

■ **SPIN**—an autorotation descent in which the model rotates about its CG location. Most models can be put into a spin, but some do it better than others (see Figure 9).

A good spin requires:
• Proper CG location.
• Plenty of control throw.

In a spin, if the wing is not completely stalled and it picks up speed in the descent, the model will enter a spiral. Before starting a spin, put the model into a slight climb to bleed off excess speed.

Figure 7 Immelmann turn.

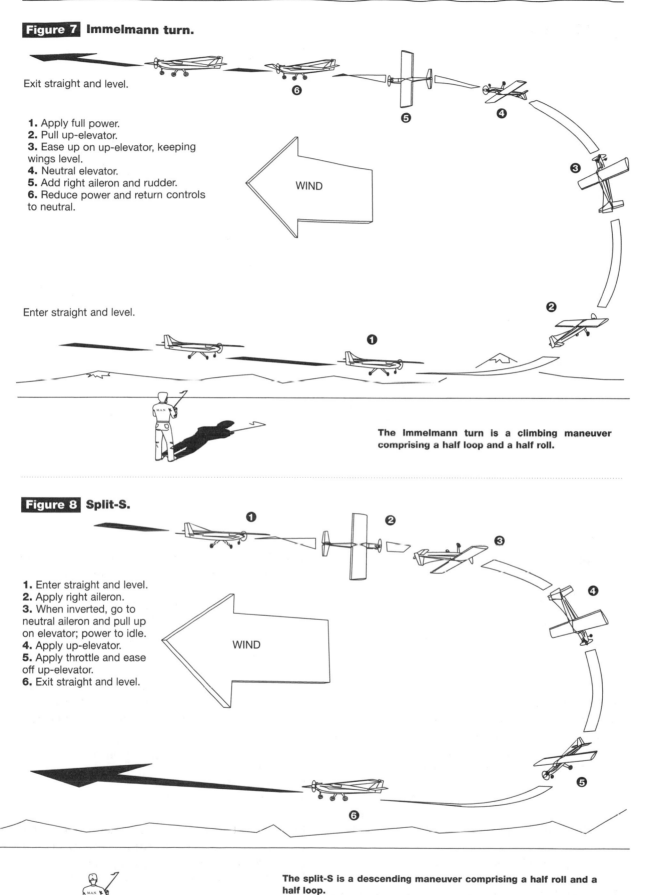

Exit straight and level.

1. Apply full power.
2. Pull up-elevator.
3. Ease up on up-elevator, keeping wings level.
4. Neutral elevator.
5. Add right aileron and rudder.
6. Reduce power and return controls to neutral.

WIND

Enter straight and level.

The Immelmann turn is a climbing maneuver comprising a half loop and a half roll.

Figure 8 Split-S.

1. Enter straight and level.
2. Apply right aileron.
3. When inverted, go to neutral aileron and pull up on elevator; power to idle.
4. Apply up-elevator.
5. Apply throttle and ease off up-elevator.
6. Exit straight and level.

WIND

The split-S is a descending maneuver comprising a half roll and a half loop.

Figure 9 **The first spin.**

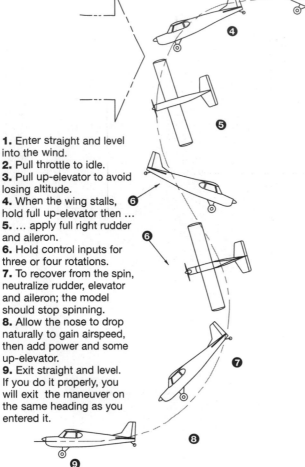

1. Enter straight and level into the wind.
2. Pull throttle to idle.
3. Pull up-elevator to avoid losing altitude.
4. When the wing stalls, hold full up-elevator then …
5. … apply full right rudder and aileron.
6. Hold control inputs for three or four rotations.
7. To recover from the spin, neutralize rudder, elevator and aileron; the model should stop spinning.
8. Allow the nose to drop naturally to gain airspeed, then add power and some up-elevator.
9. Exit straight and level. If you do it properly, you will exit the maneuver on the same heading as you entered it.

To spin:
• Climb to a very safe altitude, say 300 feet. In the event of a mishap, this altitude will allow you plenty of time to recover (especially important for your first attempt).
• Pull back on the throttle and elevator.
• When the model stalls and the nose drops past horizontal, apply full left rudder and full aileron and hold the elevator full up.
• The model should now be spinning its little heart out with its nose at about 45 degrees below the horizon. If the rotation is slow, add rudder throw, but do it a little at a time.

If the model still doesn't enter the spin properly, increase elevator throw, or add weight to the tail a little at a time to move the CG farther back until the model does spin. Don't go crazy with adding weight, or your model might become unstable and difficult to fly.

To recover from a spin (this is very easy):
• Let go of the controls! The model may rotate once or twice more, but it should recover by itself.
• Let the nose drop naturally to regain airspeed and unstall the wing.
• Gradually add up-elevator and apply some power to bring the model back to straight and level.
• Exit the spin on the same heading as you entered it but at a much lower altitude (at least, in a perfect world, you should). If the model does not stop spinning cleanly, apply slight opposite rudder and aileron to help stop its rotation.

■ **SNAP ROLL**—a "rolling" maneuver that is much faster than a roll induced by ailerons alone; many people are confused about what a true snap roll is. It is *not* a fast roll with rudder and up-elevator thrown in for good measure. For the model to truly snap roll, the wing has to first be stalled. Think of a snap roll as a fast, horizontal spin. During the maneuver, the model rotates so quickly about its CG that it is said to "snap."

To snap roll:
• Reduce power to about half throttle (some designs might need even less power), and quickly apply full up-elevator, full right rudder and aileron.
• Hold the controls for about three quarters of the snap's rotation, and then let go. The model should stop its snap roll.
• If the model doesn't rotate faster or goes into a tight barrel roll, you need more elevator travel, or you should move the CG farther aft. Depending on the model's attitude when you released the controls, you might have to modify your recovery control inputs. You want the model to end up straight and level on the same heading as it went in. The particular details of the control inputs, e.g., CG location and trim settings, will vary from model to model. Follow the guidelines given above, and you will be able to produce the best snap roll your model can perform.

By practicing aerobatic maneuvers—even the "easy" ones—you hone your piloting skills. Put purpose into your flying, and try to build on what you've learned. Improving your skills is the journey!

The Next Step

When you've flown your model for a while, you'll somehow find that you're no longer reacting to its demands but instead are in control. Rarely will its actions surprise you; in fact, you might even miss that initial feeling of being really challenged. You're ready to move on, and there's much more to learn.

Hone your piloting skills and have fun by perfecting aerobatic maneuvers, shooting touch-and-go's and making spot landings; it's even more fun if you and your friends can make it a contest. Competing at local contests and fun-flys is enjoyed as much by beginners as by more experienced pilots. If you make your main contest goals enjoyment and learning something new, you'll never be a loser. But you don't have to compete; if you find the idea stressful, who needs it?

Figure 1 **The touch-and-go**

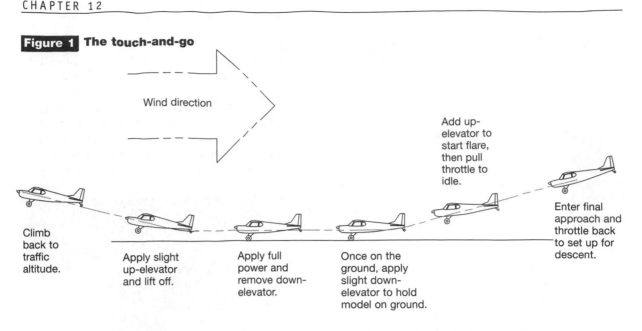

Wind direction

Add up-elevator to start flare, then pull throttle to idle.

Enter final approach and throttle back to set up for descent.

Climb back to traffic altitude.

Apply slight up-elevator and lift off.

Apply full power and remove down-elevator.

Once on the ground, apply slight down-elevator to hold model on ground.

The touch-and-go (from right to left) offers a great way to practice takeoff and landing. It also builds confidence.

TRY THE TRICKY STUFF

Touch-and-go's and spot landings are always fun no matter how long you've been flying R/C. You'll soon see that the true hotshot pilot is not the one who does triple snap rolls and eats up the sky with great abandon; the truly good pilot is the one who *always* land his models safely and precisely, no matter how short the runway is or how strong the wind is that day.

■ TOUCH-AND-GO—a great maneuver to perfect landing skills without actually ending your flight (see Figure 1). The secret to success here is to have the idle low enough to ensure that you don't have to *force* the model *onto the ground*. This, and being able to fly a consistent landing pattern pays big dividends in perfecting your landing style.

Most of us start by stubbing the prop and flipping the model over; there's rarely any real damage except to the prop—and perhaps to our egos. The next step is usually to an exciting act known as a "bounce and go." When you can consistently bring your model down without bouncing it and then take it back up to full power and climb out gracefully, you'll be ready for the next challenge: the "spot landing."

■ SPOT LANDING. The saying, "Any landing you can walk away from is a good landing," is as true in R/C flying as in full-scale aviation. In other words, if, at the end of a day at the field, you leave with the same number of model parts as you arrived with, you've had a successful day.

Spot landings train you to manage airspeed and

airplane attitude and to make full use of your peripheral vision. You learn to divide your attention between the model and the chosen landing spot. You then start to mentally "connect the dots" and are soon able to land your model just where you want it. This is very important, especially if you move on to building and flying larger, faster models. A lot of models are damaged when they flip over after running off the end of the runway.

ATTEND EVENTS

If there are any, attend fun-fly contests and fly-ins. You'll perhaps be treated to flying at a field that's bigger and more developed than your local landing patch; and you'll also enjoy seeing the efforts of other modelers. You might discover that scale, giant-scale, old-timer aircraft, or pylon racing interest you, and you'll have a chance to see these types up close and personal. And don't forget that making new friends is one of the best parts of going to flying events.

Attending an annual fun-fly or giant-scale warbird rally makes a great mini vacation. Soon, you'll know the "regulars," and attending an event will be a chance to catch up with friends as well as to fly.

As you learn to fly with more precision, the type of models you prefer will change. What's the next step? Here are some of your options:

TAKE THE NEXT STEP

■ SHOULDER-WING DESIGN—a little less stable and a bit more challenging to try after you've mastered your trainer (see Figure 2). The wing is lower, and that increases maneuverability: roll rate and

The Great Planes Ultra Sport 40 is a good low-wing sport plane. This version is an ARF.

point it, doesn't recover on its own to stable, horizontal flight, and you don't have to fight to keep it in inverted or in knife-edge flight.

■ BIGGER, FASTER DESIGN. Running a larger engine is another way to enhance performance, and then you'll probably also consider building and flying larger models. Many modelers say that bigger is better; they mean that larger

the tightness of the rolling maneuver improve. You're moving from a positively stable model to a more neutrally stable one. These models go where you point them, but they don't recover quickly by themselves.

After building and flying one or two shoulder-wing designs, you can bring a low-wing design into your hangar.

■ LOW-WING DESIGN—generally the most maneuverable and, in many ways, the easiest type of model to fly aerobatic maneuvers with. It has almost no inherent stability: it goes where you

For .60 engines, the Carl Goldberg Models low-wing Tiger 60 is a good choice. Excellent instructions and good hardware make this kit a good buy.

Figure 2 Stability in design

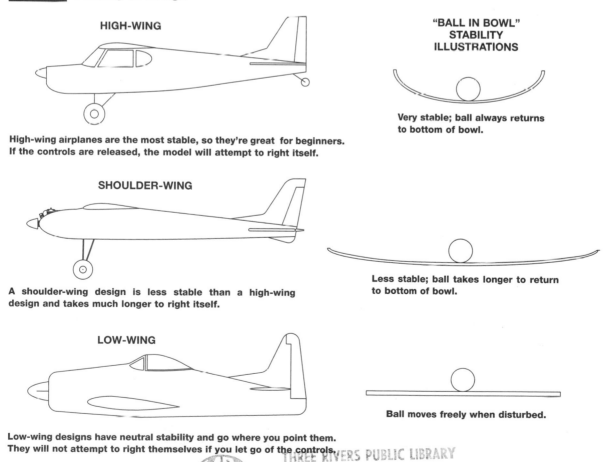

HIGH-WING

High-wing airplanes are the most stable, so they're great for beginners. If the controls are released, the model will attempt to right itself.

SHOULDER-WING

A shoulder-wing design is less stable than a high-wing design and takes much longer to right itself.

LOW-WING

Low-wing designs have neutral stability and go where you point them. They will not attempt to right themselves if you let go of the controls.

"BALL IN BOWL" STABILITY ILLUSTRATIONS

Very stable; ball always returns to bottom of bowl.

Less stable; ball takes longer to return to bottom of bowl.

Ball moves freely when disturbed.

models tend to "fly on the wing" like full-size airplanes, instead of "flying on the prop," i.e., that many "smaller" models rely heavily on engine thrust to perform.

■ **SCALE MODELING.** Precision in construction and flight are the goals of the scale modeler, and for many, modeling scale aircraft represents the absolute high point of the R/C hobby. The models look like their full-size counterparts, and their pilots learn to fly models in a "scale-like" manner. Scale-like performance is the goal. This requires homework: research and documentation of the subject aircraft—a process that can be fairly involved and entail a lot of research. Show me a dedicated scale modeler, and I'll show you a modeler who has a pretty good collection of books and magazines on full-size aircraft. It can become an obsession!

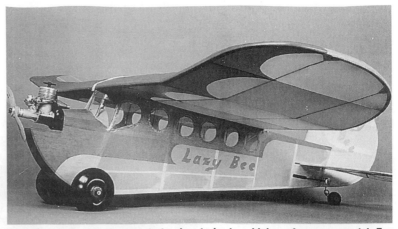

There's no rule that your next step has to be to a high-performance model. For just "plane fun-flying," the Clancy Aviation Lazy Bee is hard to beat; available in several sizes, it's a popular fun sport model.

looks, but you have only to show that your model looks like the full-scale subject, and you'll earn maximum points. After that, you earn points for flying your model in as "scale-like" a manner as you can; for example, if you fly a ¼-scale biplane, it should fly at a relatively slow speed—not at scale jet speed!

• **Sport scale.** This is what you see in all the magazines. The AMA Scale Nationals and Scale Masters and the prestigious Top Gun "invitational" are the three, top, sport-scale events in the U.S. (The rules of the latter two differ slightly from the AMA's scale competition requirements.)

Sport scale is divided into expert, sportsman and novice classes, and some events have "team scale," in which a builder and a pilot compete together. Based in France, the *Federation Aeronautique Internationale* (FAI) regulates many types of competition worldwide, including "precision scale." See how many choices you have?

Getting into scale can be easy if you choose a 3-channel sport-scale model. Here, good friends Nick Ziroli Sr. (left) and Tim Hagerty show off their 80-inch-span Taubes. Designed by Nick, these models are relatively easy to build and very easy to fly.

■ **SCALE FLYING**—exists on many levels. The best place to start is in fun scale, as the emphasis is on flying and not on building a perfect replica of a full-scale aircraft.

• **Fun scale.** For this, you need to do only minimum research and to provide the judges only with the most basic documentation (photos, model box art, drawings, etc.). "Static points" are earned for

In all categories, the models are judged in "static" and "flight" segments; the "static" judges take into account accuracy of outline, color and markings and overall craftsmanship (viewed from a distance of about 15 feet). Each pilot's static and flight scores are combined to determine the overall winner.

Flight judging involves a number of judges

Perhaps the best model for giant-scale flying is Sig's ¼-scale, clipped-wing J-3 Cub. It has a one-piece wing and can be powered by a large 2- or 4-stroke engine or a small gasoline engine.

watching the model perform on the flightline. Certain maneuvers are mandatory (e.g., takeoff, procedure turns and slow flybys); others are optional (e.g., loops, wingovers and barrel rolls). "Flight realism" is also assessed, as is the model's position during maneuvers—very important because it shows the pilot's skills. Maneuvers should start and finish immediately in front of the pilot and judges, and takeoff and landing should be straight down the runway centerline.

• **Giant scale**. Under International Miniature Aircraft Association (IMAA) rules, giant-scale models are monoplanes with wingspans of 80 inches or more and biplanes with wingspans larger than 60 inches. They commonly use gasoline engines, but many use large-displacement 2- and 4-stroke glow engines. Whereas scale modeling is very competitive, giant-scale modeling and the IMAA appeal to those who just want to enjoy flying in a non-competitive atmosphere— no contests, no trophies and no pressure. The IMAA holds rallies across the country; the annual "Rally of Giants" is held at different venues, and regardless of where you live, at some time during the year, there's probably an IMAA event not too far away.

■ **PYLON RACING**—if you enjoy speed, going fast and turning left will interest you. Pylon racing is held at many levels:
• **Quickie 500**—the simplest form. Standard shoulder-wing designs with 500 square inches of wing area and a .40-size engine compete.

Two or three pylons define the course and each pilot has a caller who tells him when to turn.

• **Quarter midget and unlimited giant scale**—the most competitive

If you like speed, pylon racing might be for you. After you've learned to fly well, a Quickie 500 sport pylon racer like the Dodger from Direct Connection R/C can open the door to true speed.

in terms of speeds and technology, and the models are as beautiful as they are fast.

The pinnacle of model racing may be giant-scale unlimited-class racing. Speeds range from 200 to over 240mph, and the average model costs more than $3,000 (but, oh, those goose bumps …!)

How about speed and giant scale? Madera-style unlimited racing is very popular but expensive. Flown on large, three-pylon courses, model speeds often exceed 200mph! Here's a good entry-level model—the G-62 powered AT-6 Texan.

Perhaps the ultimate in modeling engineering is the ducted-fan jet. Powered by a model airplane engine and a ducted-fan unit, these models can reach speeds of 150 to 200mph—a lofty speed goal, but any pilot can aspire to it.

Known as IMAC aircraft, large, powerful sport-scale models fly scale aerobatic sequences. Here, John Kohler shows off his Tucker Special biplane next to the full-size Sean Tucker 1-800-COLLECT aircraft the model is scaled after.

the best compete.

When you're proficient enough for aerobatics, you might enjoy competing in International Miniature Aerobatics Club (IMAC) events—regional gatherings of pilots who try to outperform one another flying basic aerobatic routines with scale aerobatic aircraft.

DIFFERENT STROKES

The variety of aircraft to choose from is huge and includes ducted-fan jets, electric-powered aircraft, sailplanes and slope-soarers, all with their own organizations and competitions.

Biplanes, racers and WW I and WW II warbirds and beautiful, clas-

■ **PRECISION AEROBATICS**—very popular all over the USA. "Aerial ballet" best describes this event. Precision in every maneuver is scored. Their tail moments are long and their airfoils are symmetrical, so they fly inverted (upside-down) as well as they do upright. Vertical performance is impressive, as few maneuvers are done in a straight horizontal line.

The best-known precision aerobatic competition in the country is the Tournament of Champions (TOC), which is generally held every two years in Las Vegas, NV. The models are almost half the size of full-size aerobatic aircraft such as the Extra 300, CAP 232 and Giles 200.

Computer-radio technology contributes a great deal to the pilots' being able to execute the type of maneuvers seen at the TOC. Vertical hovers, knife-edge loops and vertical torque rolls are typical. It's both exciting and humbling to watch the best of

For a different kind of piloting challenge, trade your wings for rotors and try your hand at helicopters. The Hirobo Shuttle (shown here with Phyllis Bell) is popular with beginners. It comes in several versions—ARF to basic kit and even a high-performance version.

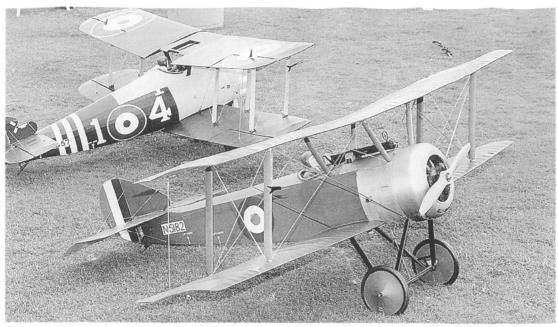

Tom Polapink's Sopwith Snipe (background) and Kim Foster's Sopwith Pup at the Top Gun Invitational international scale competition.

sic, civilian aircraft are all part of the R/C modeling scene.

Whether you like pattern, giant-scale warbirds or just big sport models, you'll soon learn that the sky

A scene from the giant-scale fly-in, Warbirds over Delaware. No competition here!

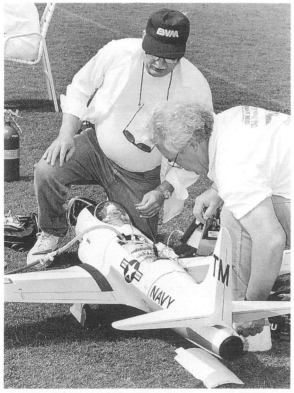

Bob Violett (left), founder of Bob Violett Models (ducted-fan specialists) and modeler Jerry Caudle prepare to start a BVM turbine-powered P-80 at Top Gun.

is the limit; if it flies, you can model it. No one was ever born a hotshot pilot; we all start at the same level, and we all learn the same basic maneuvers. The only difference between you and the impressive expert pilot you saw at the flying field is practice.

But whatever the direction of your next step, remember to start where you feel comfortable and then build on that. You can go anywhere you want if you map out *your* best route.

13

Prop Talk

Editor's note: this chapter comprises three very recent articles on propellers that were published in Model Airplane News *magazine in response to the many requests readers constantly make for information on this subject.*

Written by Chris Chianelli (senior editor of that magazine) and contributing writers Dave Gierke (top model engine authority and author of "2-Stroke Glow Engines for R/C Aircraft" published by Air Age Inc.) and Jim Newman (noted illustrator and aviation historian), the articles contain information that will be of great value as you progress beyond the novice level, so they are reprinted here as they appeared in the magazine. Chris and Dave address the issue of matching props to airframes; Jim provides a detailed overview of propeller balancing, care and handling.

M ost powered R/C airplanes are moved through the air by propellers, but the importance of selecting, balancing and caring for these props is too often overlooked; in fact, most of us will readily admit that "prop thought" isn't high on our list of priorities. As a beginner, you might find this chapter more than you're immediately ready to cope with, but when you start to fly, you'll soon realize why we include this information.

Follow the advice given here, and not only will your models fly better, but you will also have a safer and more enjoyable time at the flying field—and perhaps become the local club's "prop guru!"

THE PROPER PROP

by Chris Chianelli

The topic of propping an airframe, and not the engine, is so important—and so often misunderstood. I'm often asked a question to which, without more information, I'm unable to give a meaningful answer. That question is, "Chris, which prop should I run on my .25, .45 or .60-size brand-X engine?" The question that *should* be asked is, "Which prop is appropriate for my model's airframe?" This is why engine manufacturers often recommend a range of props of various diameters and pitches in the instructions for one of their engines of a specific displacement.

Let's take, for example, a strong, twin-ball-bearing sport .45 and consider it on three vastly different airframes with broadly disparate wing areas, wing loadings and drag factors. Let's look first at a very dirty, high-drag Fokker triplane with 750 square inches of wing area, then a super-clean, low-drag Ultra Sport with retracts and 550 square inches of wing area and, falling between these two, a medium-drag Spacewalker with 650 square inches of wing area.

To keep things simple, let's assume each weighs in at 5.5 pounds (88 ounces, for a total weight of 100 ounces when the approximate 12 ounces of a sport .45-size engine is added). This gives each airframe a power loading (power-to-weight ratio) of 222 ounces per cubic inch. The preceding is one of the factors designers consider when determining the correct engine displacement for a certain model to ensure it will be adequately powered. But this still tells us nothing about which prop will make best use of the engine's power when considering a specific airframe's unique drag and lift characteristics.

There's one thing that, for now, you'll just have to accept on trust: ideally, a generic prop with a given pitch rotating at a given rpm will attempt to achieve a specific airspeed (in level flight) at which the engine/prop combination will be operating at peak efficiency. This efficiency will be realized if, and only if, the airframe it is matched with will allow it to do so.

To illustrate the point, let's suppose we have a 10x9 prop turning at 12,000rpm on our sport .45 engine. Using the nomograph (see Figure 1 at right) of Andy Lennon's book, "R/C Model Aircraft Design," the estimated speed this pitch/rpm com-

bination would produce is approximately 125mph; that is, if the airframe in question and its inherent drag will allow.

Now let's move this spinning prop to the nose of the Fokker triplane. Obviously, with the drag presented by a .45-size model with three wings, a round cowl, fixed landing gear and cabane and

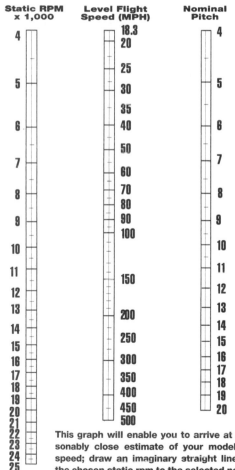

Figure 1

Static RPM x 1,000	Level Flight Speed (MPH)	Nominal Pitch
4	18.3 / 20	4
5	25 / 30 / 35	5
6	40 / 50	6
7	60	7
8	70 / 80	8
9	90 / 100	9
10		10
11	150	11
12		12
13	200	13
14	250	14
15	300	15
16		16
17	350	17
18	400	18
19	450	19
20 / 21 / 22 / 23 / 24 / 25	500	20

This graph will enable you to arrive at a reasonably close estimate of your model's top speed; draw an imaginary straight line from the chosen static rpm to the selected nominal pitch, and estimated flight speed will be identified in the middle column.

interplane struts, it's never going to fly anywhere near 125mph. If you attempt to force the issue in a power-on dive, dangerous control-surface flutter would surely result. If, by wizardry, the Fokker's engine displacement were magically doubled in the middle of this already daunting power-dive, the poor little triplane just might self-destruct in a mass of airborne confetti faster than you can say "VNE" (velocity never exceed).

The Fokker's inherent drag will not permit it to reach sufficient speed, so it won't allow the engine to unload to sufficiently high rpm levels to reach its optimum torque-band range. Simply stated, the engine is too "loaded" under these conditions.

Conversely, let's assume the Fokker's airframe allows a top speed of only 60mph. Again, if we used Andy's chart, we'd find that in the ballpark of 12,000rpm, a 4-inch pitch would match this speed nicely. Since the pitch has now been drastically decreased, we must now manipulate the diameter to keep the engine turning in the 12,000rpm range. A 12-inch diameter will probably do nicely. If the 12-inch diameter happens to reduce the rpm level to 11,500, for argument's sake, this would bring the speed to about 55mph, which would still be correct for a .40-size model of this type. At the very least, a 12x4 prop would be an excellent starting point for the Fokker. Using the 10x9 prop, or anything close to it would be, in a sense, kind of like driving uphill in a pickup truck loaded with firewood in fourth gear.

The other side of the picture, of course, would be to put the .45 engine/10x9 prop combination on a clean design like a .40- to .45-size Ultra Sport. With retracts, this airframe would have no problem whatsoever attaining 130mph. This would allow the engine to go ahead and unload at 12,000rpm. So a 10x9, or possibly an 11x8 would be a good match. In terms of lift, drag and top speed, the Spacewalker would fall somewhere between the Ultra Sport and Fokker, making an 11x6 prop a good starting point for this design. At 12,000rpm, the 11x6 would be looking in the neighborhood of 80mph—a very comfortable neighborhood for a Spacewalker.

These are some practical examples that make use of Andy's ingenious nomograph, with some empirical thought added to the mix regarding the overall "dragginess" of your R/C airplane. If you'd like a little more technical insight to nail your prop selection dead-on, the following information by Dave Gierke gives an easy-to-use arithmetical tool you'll find very useful during testing at the field. You'll truly be an expert, not just sound like one (like that guy in every club who wears a windsock beanie and

mirrored sunglasses, walks the flightline and bestows advice—but never flies).

THE LOAD FACTOR FORMULA
by Dave Gierke

You're at the flying field trimming out a shiny new sport model when one of your more experienced flying buddies asks, "Are you at full throttle? The engine doesn't sound like it's turning fast enough. I think you're using too much prop. Maybe you should try one that doesn't load the engine as much."

Too much prop? Loading the engine too much? To many modelers, these terms are meaningless—something for the experts to fuss about. After all, engines are engines, right? Fasten a prop to the shaft, fuel it, fire it up and fly. What could be simpler?

Why is it important to match the propeller to the engine? If you read the instructions that accompany your engine, the manufacturer probably recommends a size—right? In many cases, this prop will put you in the ballpark for a trainer-type model. But what happens if your model is somewhat different from the hypothetical trainer? What if it's a biplane? It may be heavier, generate more air drag and fly slower, or it might require a propeller with more diameter and less pitch. A lightweight monoplane with a relatively thin wing, streamlined fuselage, wing fairings and a low-drag cowl will probably produce less drag, fly faster and demand a prop with less diameter and more pitch. How do you determine which prop to use?

■ **WHICH PROP SHOULD I USE?** For a given engine displacement and horsepower, there are propellers that are either too big or too small to function properly. Some foul up the engine's operation; others are inadequate to fly the model; some are guilty of both inadequacies. If the prop is too large, it has too much diameter and/or pitch. Changes in diameter affect engine load the most. Oversize props force the engine to operate too slowly, and this limits the horsepower needed to fly the airplane and invites overheating—especially with 2-stroke-cycle engines. Experience has shown that most 2-stroke engines abhor being operated below 10,000rpm at wide-open throttle without special modifications.

Engines outfitted with props that have excessive pitch and marginal low-speed thrust production may not be able to achieve minimum takeoff speed: they run out of runway! After taking off into the wind, propellers with insufficient pitch may not maintain the minimum flight speed required to avoid the dreaded stall spin. In general, undersize propellers allow over-speeding, increase fuel consumption and reduce engine longevity.

Most fliers learn about propeller requirements by trial and error, or they copy what their buddies use, and sometimes, that's a good idea, especially with a new airplane. But after the bugs have been worked out, many desire improved performance: better climbing ability (vertical performance?), top speed, or takeoff acceleration. Sorry! Unless you increase the engine's horsepower, you probably can't realize these attributes simultaneously. Without changing the power, prop selection becomes a compromise. A shorter ground run prior to takeoff is accomplished with a lower-pitch prop, resulting in improved acceleration—at the expense of reduced top speed. Top speed can be improved dramatically with a higher-pitch prop at the expense of a much longer takeoff run and reduced vertical performance. Most sport fliers prefer a performance smorgasbord: a little of each, thank you!

■ **UNDERSTAND THE NUMBERS.** If you like to experiment, the following technique allows you to manipulate flight performance incrementally—not wildly, or from one extreme to another. This strategy allows you to change (or modify) the propeller in terms of its diameter, pitch, or both, while maintaining or selectively changing the load on the

engine. Sounds complicated but you'll find it really isn't.

Propeller load and engine rpm are inversely related: as load increases, rpm decrease and vice versa. Load is represented by the propeller; change propeller size, and load is changed. By using the propeller load factor (PLF) formula, $Lprop = D^2(P)$, incremental propeller load changes can be determined and applied to the engine/model combination.
• Lprop = PLF.
• D = diameter.
• P = pitch.
For example, if the sport model we're taking as our example was fitted with a 10x8 propeller, PLF would be 800 (10x10x8 = 800). Because propeller rpm increase as PLF decreases, we need to find a prop with a number that's less than 800. I have compiled a list of APC sport propellers and calculated their PLF to illustrate the technique:

Linear sizes	Rearranged by load	PLF
9x6	11x3	363
9x7	10x4	400
9x8	11x4	484
9x9	9x6	486
9x10	10x5	500
10x4	9x7	567
10x5	10x6	600
10x6	11x5	605
10x7	9x8	648
10x8	10x7	700
10x9	11x6	726
11x3	9x9	729
11x4	10x8	800
11x5	9x10	810
11x6	11x7	847
11x7	10x9	900
11x8	11x8	968

From the list, the next smallest PLF is 729 and is represented by the 9x9 propeller. This prop allows engine rpm to increase and would generate higher top speed at the expense of a longer, slower takeoff run. Climb performance would probably also suffer. The 11x6 propeller with a similar PLF (726), offers almost the same load as the 9x9 but provides better takeoff and climb performance while sacrificing some top speed. Another possibility would be the 10x7 (PLF 700). It allows the engine to speed up a bit more than the 9x9 and 11x6 while allowing an in-between top speed and takeoff potential.

Notice that I haven't included propellers from a

variety of manufacturers on the PLF list. Because blade shape, area, airfoils and pitch generation all have an effect on load, you should limit PLF to families of propellers from specific manufacturers.

Although the PLF system doesn't provide an initial propeller size for your engine/model combination, it points you in the right direction based on your observations of engine rpm, takeoff distance, climb rate and flight speed (among other factors). You and your friends can now make objective evaluations of a model's performance based on how the engine and propeller are functioning. There may not be agreement, but you now have a tool that tells you where you are and in which direction you should head.

PROPER PROPS

by Jim Newman

Like most modelers, the care and feeding of propellers was never high on my list of priorities. I did as everyone else did: I walked into the hobby shop, handed over my money and walked out with a wooden propeller clutched in my grubby little fist.

I promptly attached that propeller to my greasy diesel engine and flew the aircraft at the first opportunity. The only props I ever finished and balanced were those on my rubber-powered models, and that was because when I started modeling, we all made our own. Ready-made propellers just did not exist.

Some years later, a couple of events really brought home to me the importance of balancing propellers. The first happened when I was in the Royal Air Force. We were in the process of accepting the very elegant Bristol Britannia airliner into service when its propeller manufacturer offered us the chance to see how its props were made. I suppose this was to establish consumer confidence in the product and, in retrospect, it was pleasant to sit between those four big Bristol Proteus turboprops feeling fairly comfortable in the knowledge that the "airscrews" (the term of that era) were not suffering from metal worm and were unlikely to depart for places distant.

During our walk through the shops, we saw one of our props in the balancing stand, which, because of its size, was half in a big, 12-foot-deep trench in the shop floor. The "boffin," as technicians were then known, was nattily attired in the obligatory long white lab coat with dress slide rule and pencil in its top pocket, and he droned on about the standards to which they balanced their beautiful, hollow-aluminum props and the reasons why they went to such trouble—not the least of which was to ensure that the poor propeller shaft wouldn't give up the ghost at 30,000 feet (no argument from me

or the rest of the crew on that one!) None of us relished the idea of our fuselage being treated as a giant salami by an errant propeller; it would create a horrendous draft for those sitting in the back—not to mention consternation among those up front who would discover that the folks at the rear had decided to go their own sweet way.

To emphasize his point, our mentor produced a 10-shilling note from his pocket, snapped it taut between the fingers of both hands and brandished it high for all to see. He then creased it across the middle and laid it over one blade: the huge propeller dutifully and gracefully rotated in the jig while our boffin—now smiling smugly all around—quite forgot about the sizable portion of his pay that had slithered off the now sloping blade and had fluttered to the bottom of the pit!

Anyway, his point about delicate balance was not lost on us, and we departed for our base, secure in the knowledge that 10 shillings will cause a propeller of humongous proportions to rotate—knowledge that, no doubt, would give us all renewed confidence the next time we were crossing the Med en route for Aden.

Some years later, I put in quite a few hours in a motor glider. In addition to the fact that wisdom dictated the wearing of ear plugs (noise was a characteristic of the machine) was that everything, but everything, vibrated enough to rattle the change in our pockets and the fillings in our teeth.

In a real rash of enthusiasm one weekend, however—and hastened by the sight of the fiberglass covering separating from the blades—I removed the prop and set about refinishing it. In short, I completely stripped each blade, made airfoil templates of each and then compared them. To my surprise, I found that the airfoil of one blade was quite different in shape and thickness from its mate on the opposite side of the hub! Having persuaded the two blades into some semblance of likeness, I reglassed and primed them, then sprayed them with HobbyPoxy silver.

At every step of the way, from the moment I started to correct the airfoil sections, I took great care to keep the prop in balance so that I would not have to do a massive balancing operation on completion; this saved me a lot of grief and hard work in the end. I balanced the prop on a pinpoint balancing device made by a local machinist. Glued to the top of the balancer was a bull's-eye bubble level that made it very easy to detect which blade and which edge of it was heavy. "Which edge?" you ask incredulously? Read on!

After reinstalling the prop on the airplane and carefully tracking it, i.e., ensuring that one propeller tip faithfully followed exactly the same path as the other, I found that the engine gave 200 more rpm on takeoff and would easily exceed the tachometer red line if I did not keep an attentive eye on it.

In short, the propeller was so much more efficient that it could have done with a couple of inches more in pitch, and we would have benefited from a higher cruise speed. Obviously, not all of that gain came from the balancing, but it does give you some idea of its importance. The other major benefit was that the airplane seemed to be 50 percent quieter in the cockpit. The instrument needles and the panel, too, placidly stayed where they should be; the tingle in my feet caused by the resonating rudder pedals subsided; and the canopy no longer rattled like a jack hammer.

Figure 1

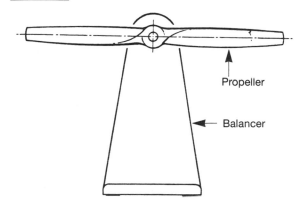

Horizontal balance; prop is only 50 percent balanced.

■ **BALANCE FOR MODELERS.** With the advent of super-efficient, model-size propeller balancers, we can easily balance our props. My balancer is one of the original, beautifully made High Point devices now available from Robart. Another good balancer, I imagine (I haven't used one), is the magnetic balancer from Top Flite. With this tool, there can't be any significant friction because one end of the pointed spindle rests against a powerful magnet while the other hangs in midair!

With the propeller mounted on the balancer's spindle, it will probably rest more or less horizontal. My friend Bill called me into his shop one day and proudly showed me how his propeller rested horizontally across the balancer, as shown in Figure 1. He spent a long time on that, he said, so I just hated to burst his bubble. "Sorry, Bill," I said, as gently as I could, "but it is only about 50-percent balanced. If that propeller stops horizontal with the same edge of the blades facing downward every time, its bottom edges are heavy. A balanced pro-

Figure 2

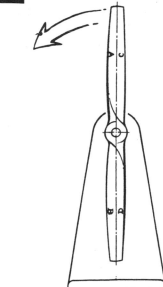

If a vertical prop acts as indicated, edge "A" is heavy.

peller should stop and remain anywhere on the circle without any tendency to rotate at all."

In this particular instance, both of the lower edges were heavy and should have been sanded on their aft faces; the propeller should have been given trial swings every now and again to see where it came to rest.

It helps considerably to mark the leading and trailing edges of the blades "A," "B," "C" and "D." Having done that, set the propeller vertical on the balancer as shown in Figure 2. If, for example, the A-C blade falls counterclockwise, edge A is the heavy one and its aft face should be sanded. Similarly, if the propeller rotates clockwise, as shown in Figure 3, you can assume that edge C is heavy and it, too, should be sanded on its aft face.

Eventually, you will reach the situation shown in Figure 4: the propeller comes to a stop on the diagonal. With this propeller, edge D consistently stops in the lower left quadrant, so its aft face should be lightly sanded and it should then be given a few trial spins to see whether there is a consistent pattern in its resting place. If it consistently stops with edge B in the lower right quadrant (Figure 5), the aft face of B should be sanded and the trial spins repeated.

When the propeller has been fully statically balanced, it will stop randomly at points all around the circle (Figure 6).

Now you apply protective coats of urethane varnish, or epoxy and recheck the balance after the finish has fully set. In most cases, a few strokes of fine sandpaper will restore the balance. More often than not, a spot or two of the finish at the end or

Figure 3

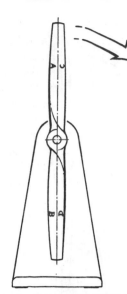

If the prop rotates clockwise, edge "C" is heavy.

Figure 4

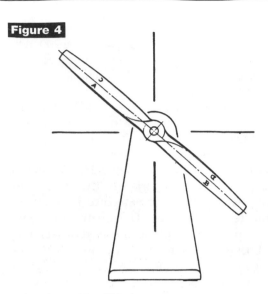

Here, edge "D" is still heavy.

Figure 5

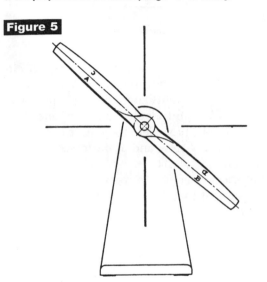

Here, the edge "B" needs to be sanded.

Figure 6

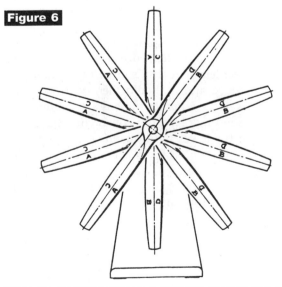

When the properly balanced, a prop will come to rest at random positions.

at the appropriate edge of one blade will accomplish the same thing, and if you are balancing two or three propellers, it is amazing how fast you can do it, because most leave the factory pretty well in balance.

Molded, glass-reinforced nylon props can be treated in the same way as wooden ones, but a good buffing is all that is required to restore the gloss after sanding, and for this, a regular metal polish on a soft cloth works wonders.

■ **VISIBILITY AND SAFETY.** I once saw a picture of the front of a model with a large circular-saw blade bolted to the propeller shaft! I thought that was a very clever and highly effective illustration of how we should view propellers. I get the impression that, since the advent of those razor-sharp, reinforced-nylon props, prop-related hand injuries have become more horrific, therefore, total concentration when going through starting and launching procedures is mandatory. I will not dwell on the handling aspects—it has been done many times elsewhere—but I will offer suggestions on enhancing prop visibility while the engine is running.

In full-size aviation, prop tips are painted bright yellow or, occasionally, white. You could not do better than imitate this practice and paint $5/8$ inch (16mm) of each blade tip yellow or white. While the propeller is spinning, this shows up as a yellow or white circle and thus defines the perimeter of the propeller arc. Of course, if you are in the habit of reaching through the propeller arc to the needle valve, you're beyond help!

Some time ago, following the addition of turbine-powered aircraft to its inventory, the Royal Air

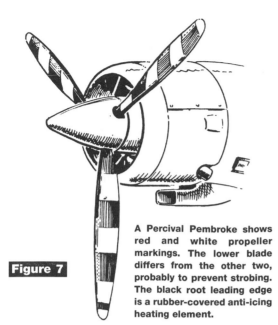

Figure 7

A Percival Pembroke shows red and white propeller markings. The lower blade differs from the other two, probably to prevent strobing. The black root leading edge is a rubber-covered anti-icing heating element.

Force carried out extensive research into prop visibility. Turboprop aircraft have their own unique problem for ground crews. The engine is operating at 90 percent of its power all the time, and thrust is varied by changing prop pitch. Consequently, that prop is spinning at very high rpm while the aircraft is on the ground, and the prop disk is all but invisible.

To compound the problem, from certain angles, the power unit is barely audible, and only when you're edge-on to the prop disk do you hear the characteristic roar off the tips and from the residual

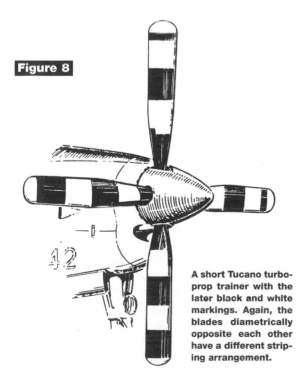

Figure 8

A short Tucano turbo-prop trainer with the later black and white markings. Again, the blades diametrically opposite each other have a different striping arrangement.

thrust of the turbine exhaust. By then, it is too late for any daydreaming, wandering soul ....

In an effort to reduce the number of sliced, diced and chipped mechanics, the RAF evolved highly effective prop markings comprising a series of red and white stripes (mostly of equal width) across the blades' forward faces—somewhat jarring to the senses of us old-fashioned traditionalists who prefer our props to look like props, and on a model, that scheme would be eye-catching. The net effect was that, when the engine was running, you saw highly obvious of red and white concentric circles, and the outermost circle—the prop tips—were white.

You could always tell when things were a little

Figure 9

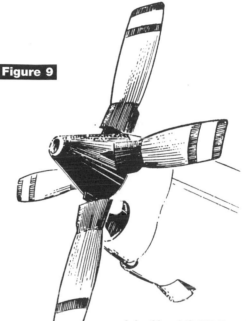

A Lockheed C.130 Hercules with gray blades and red and white striped tips only. The white band is approximately twice the width of the red bands. In all three examples, the rear faces of the blades are black.

slow in the halls of the Ministry of Defense (Air) in London; that's when they refilled the old teapot and sat around the table to decide on sweeping changes in colors and markings—presumably to give the lads something to do when the weather is bad and there's no flying going on!

Sure enough, after all the props had been painted red and white, somebody must have got a good deal on black paint at Woolworth's, because the red and white stripes suddenly became black and white were declared the appropriate colors ! On the other hand, it's likely that one of the committee threw a fit because he still had red paint left, and to appease him, some aircraft now have their propeller tips painted in

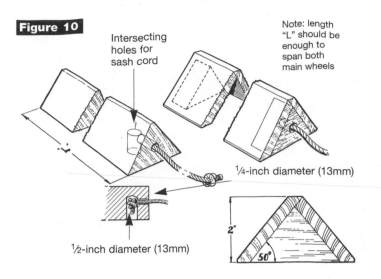

Figure 10

Intersecting holes for sash cord

Note: length "L" should be enough to span both main wheels

¼-inch diameter (13mm)

½-inch diameter (13mm)

2"

50°

two red stripes with a broad white one in between …! Figures 7, 8 and 9 show the progression of their lordship's deliberations over tea and crumpets.

■ **GROUND SAFETY.** When starting and running any model, use a chock; I can't recommend this too highly. For several years, I have used a 1½x20-inch (38x510mm) chock (Figure 10). Actually, 2x20 inches (50x510mm) would be better, but I used the material I had to hand. Attach a light, 60-inch (152cm) rope to one end of the chock, and paint it with bright yellow urethane paint. I made mine using a table saw, but if you don't have access to one, you can make a chock out of lengths of flat lumber with triangular ends.

Before starting your engine, put the chock in front of the main wheels and lay the rope out toward a convenient wingtip. When you're ready to taxi away, grasp the end of the rope and smoothly pull the chock clear. *Do not jerk it away;* you might snag it on the grass and flip the chock into the propeller arc. For engine runs, I use two denim bags joined by a webbing strap and filled with old nuts and bolts. I lay the strap across the rear fuselage, and the weight of the bags keeps the tail down (just as we did in the RAF when running up Spitfires).

I felt a little self-conscious when I first showed up at the Sundowner's field with my chock, but a few favorable comments soon dispelled my embarrassment. In the past 10 years, it has saved me from serious injury only once; nevertheless, as far as I am concerned, it has paid for itself handsomely and has been worth the effort of always installing it immediately after parking. What happened? Oh, you must have seen it at your field a dozen times. Kneeling in front of my Fox .60-powered Telemaster, after starting up, I stretched out my

hand to bring the throttle stick back. Instead, I brushed the stick with the back of my hand and knocked it almost wide open; the aircraft lunged against the chock, which stopped it and prevented my knees and thighs from being seriously lacerated. Yes! I *do* move to the rear of the aircraft before touching the needle—*always*. As a freelance illustrator and draftsman, I am extremely conscious of the fact that if I damage my hands, we don't eat.

■ **DON'T MODIFY PROPS!** From time to time, we see articles on how to modify props to create four-blade versions. Do not do this for a flying prop! Sawing halfway through the hubs of two props and then making a lap joint (as I saw in one magazine) is *not* the way to do it. The stresses on the prop hub (in particular, the tensile loads) are tremendous.

In general, *don't do anything to propeller hubs* other than to carefully smooth them with fine sandpaper. The prop drive washers fitted to some larger engines have two protruding pegs and the hubs must be drilled to accept them. The recommendation of knowledgeable people is that you remove the pegs. Props are meant to be driven by the friction between the prop hub and the drive washer, and if your prop persistently slips, the best remedy is to cut a washer out of 400-grit sandpaper, use CA to glue them back to back—grit side out, of course—and slip this washer onto the shaft before you install the prop. It will eliminate any chance of its slipping. Drilling holes to accept those pegs will increase the risk of splitting propellers end to end and throwing the blades, and we've had a couple of documented cases of that recently.

When tightening the shaft nut on a wooden prop, do not tighten it so much that it crushes the wood because this prop damage creates stress risers. You will also find that, having been crushed, the prop nut will soon need to be tightened again … and again … and again. Use the old sandpaper trick and a self-locking nut on the engine shaft.

I can't understand why manufacturers do not provide self-locking nuts and slightly longer crankshafts. If they are to remain effective, nylon-insert locking nuts should be replaced regularly; you can't count the cost of safety. I know that Harry Higley and Sons Inc. offer a thin locking nut for propeller shafts that, when tightened against the existing nut, prevents that sudden prop spin-off. Harry's thin nut should be readily available through your local hobby store. Safety first!

Glossary of Aviation Terms

Adverse yaw. When turning an airplane using only ailerons, the drag of the lowered aileron is greater than that of the raised aileron; this extra drag tends to yaw the airplane in a direction that's the opposite of what the pilot intends.

Aerobatics. Maneuvers that involve bank and pitch angles in excess of 60 degrees.

Aerodynamics. The dynamics of bodies relative to gases—especially the interaction of solid objects moving within the atmosphere.

Aileron. A hinged or movable portion of an airplane's wing (usually at the trailing edge); primarily used to induce a roll.

Airfoil. A part or surface, e.g., wing, prop blade, aileron or rudder, that's designed (shape, orientation, etc.) to control aircraft stability, direction, lift, thrust, or propulsion.

Angle of attack. (AoA). The acute angle between the wing chord line and the relative airflow.

Auxiliary channel. Any radio-channel function other than one of the four basic channels—aileron, rudder, elevator and throttle.

Base leg. The part of the landing pattern that's at 90 degrees to the final approach.

Bulkhead. A solid, vertical piece of wood inside a fuselage that helps to give it shape and rigidity.

Center of gravity (CG). A model airplane's balance point.

Climb out. To gain altitude after takeoff.

Control linkage. Metal rods or plastic tubes that connect servos to control surfaces.

Control surface. A movable airfoil that can be controlled by the pilot to change the aircraft's attitude.

Crab. To point the model's nose into a crosswind by using the rudder to move the model sideways and prevent it from being blown off-course.

Crosswind. Wind blowing across the takeoff run or the model's flight path.

Crosswind leg. Portion of the traffic pattern at 90 degrees to either the upwind or downwind legs; directly opposite the base leg.

Dead-stick landing. A landing with the engine stopped.

Doubler. A section of balsa or plywood added to the inside of a fuselage side to strengthen it.

Drag. Air resistance that slows the airplane.

Elevator. A movable control surface—usually on the horizontal stabilizer—that's used to control the model's pitch attitude.

Final approach. The portion of the landing pattern that starts from the 90-degree turn from the base leg and is followed by the landing.

Flare. A slow, smooth transition from a normal approach attitude to a landing attitude.

Former. An open, vertical piece of wood inside the fuselage that helps to give it shape and rigidity.

Fuel mixture. The mixture of air and fuel drawn into the engine through the carburetor.

Fuselage. The main body of the airplane.

Ground effect. A reduction of induced drag's downwash caused by the downwash hitting the ground sooner than expected; it allows the plane to gain a little extra lift.

Headwind. Wind blowing straight at a model (parallel to its line of flight).

Heading. The direction the model travels over the ground. Not the direction the model is pointing.

Horizontal stabilizer. Flight surface that supports the elevator; also stabilizes the model in pitch.

Induced drag. The drag that is a direct result of the production of lift.

Landing gear (conventional). An airplane's wheels, axles and supporting structure. Conventional landing gear is a tail-dragger configuration.

Leading edge (LE). The foremost edge of an airfoil or prop blade.

Lean mixture. An air/fuel mixture setting that contains more air than the engine requires to run efficiently.

Lift. A created aerodynamic force that is equal to or greater than the weight of the airplane and acts in opposition to the force of gravity.

Longeron. A long, square or triangular balsa "stick" that runs from nose to tail to strengthen the fuselage.

Longitudinal axis. An imaginary straight line that runs through the fuselage from nose to tail and through the model's CG on the same plane.

Moment (nose moment, tail moment). Refers to a distance on a model forward or aft of the balance point.

Nose-heavy. A condition in which a model's CG (balance point) is too far forward.

Over-control. Excessive control inputs that overcompensate for unwanted model movement.

Parasite drag. The sum of pressure and skin-friction drag.

Pressurized fuel system. A fuel-tank setup in which the vent tube is connected to the pressure nipple on the muffler. The pressure from the muffler pressurizes the fuel tank and helps pump the fuel to the carb.

Receiver (RX). The part of the radio system that receives the radio signal sent by the transmitter.

Ribs. Vertical portions of the wing's structure that give it its contour.

Rich mixture. An air/fuel mixture that contains more fuel than the engine requires to run efficiently.

Rudder. Vertical, hinged control surface that controls yaw.

Servo. Electromechanical device that moves the control surfaces.

Positive stability. The natural tendency of a model to return to a straight and level condition.

Stall. The point at which the wing experiences a loss of lift; the aircraft will tend to drop.

Stringer. A thin, stick-like length of wood that supports a model's covering. Similar to a longeron but does not significantly contribute to the model's strength.

Symmetrical airfoil. An airfoil that has the same curve on its top and bottom surfaces.

Tail-heavy. A condition in which the model's CG (balance point) is too far aft.

Taxi. To move the model along on the ground under its own power.

Thrust. A generated force that is required to overcome the natural resistance of drag.

Torque. The force created by the engine spinning the propeller; it will turn an airplane to its left.

Trailing edge (TE). The aft edge of an airfoil or prop blade.

Transmitter (TX). The part of the radio system that sends the radio signal to the RX.

Trike (tricycle landing gear). Landing gear that includes a nose gear and two main gear.

Trim. To adjust a model's control surfaces to obtain the balanced flight performance you want.

Upwind leg. First portion of the landing pattern directly opposite the downwind leg and 90 degrees to the crosswind leg.

Vertical fin. A fixed vertical airfoil that gives directional stability, i.e., it reduces the tendency to yaw about the vertical axis.

Wing spar. Runs from wingtip to wingtip; the wing's main horizontal member; gives the wing its strength.

Yaw. The left and right movement of the aircraft's nose about the vertical axis.

Y-harness. A Y-shaped wire with one input connection and two output connections.

Z-bend. The simplest way to connect the pushrod to a control horn or servo arm. Shaped like a "Z."

Useful Addresses and Websites

Academy of Model Aeronautics (AMA), 5151 East Memorial Dr., Muncie, IN 47302; (765) 287-1256; membership (800) 435-9262.

Ace Hobby Distributors, 116 W. 19th St., Higginsville, MO 64037-0472; (800) 322-7121; (660) 584-7121; fax (660) 584-7766; www.acehobby.com

Air Age Inc., 100 East Ridge, Ridgefield, CT 06877; (203) 431-900; fax (203) 431-3000; to subscribe to *Model Airplane News*, call (800) 827-0323 (in USA and Canada), or (815) 734-1116; www.airage.com

Airtronics, 1185 Stanford Court, Anaheim, CA 92805; (714) 978-1895; fax (714) 978-1540.

Altech Marketing, P.O. Box 7182, Edison, NJ 08818-7182; (732) 225-6144.; fax (732) 225-0091; www.modelrec.com

APC Props; distributed by Landing Products, 122 Harter Ave., Woodland, CA 95776; (916) 661-0399.

AristoCraft; distributed by Polk's Model Craft Hobbies Inc., 346 Bergen Ave., Jersey City, NJ 07304; (201) 332-8100; fax (201) 332-0521.

AstroFlight Inc., 13311 Beach Ave., Marina del Rey, CA 90292; (310) 821-6242; fax (310) 822-6637; www.astroflight.com

Balsa USA, P.O. Box 164, Marinette, WI 54143; (906) 863-6421; fax (906) 863-5878.

Bob Violett Models (BVM), 170 State Rd. 419; Winter Springs, FL 32708; (407) 327-6333; fax (407) 327-5020; www.bvmjets.com

BTE: Bruce Tharpe Engineering, 13555 E. Evans Creek Rd., Rogue River, OR 97537; (541) 582-1708.

Carl Goldberg Models, 4734 W. Chicago Ave., Chicago, IL 60651; (312) 626-9550; fax (312) 626-9566.

CGM: Carl Goldberg Models (address above).

Clancy Aviation, P.O. Box 4125, Mesa, AZ 85210-1317; (602) 649-1534.

Coverite; distributed by Great Planes (address below).

Cox Hobbies, 350 W. Rincon St., Corona CA 91720; (909) 278-7282.

Dave Brown Products, 4560 Layhigh Rd., Hamilton, OH 45013; (513) 738-1576; fax (513) 738-0152; wwwdbproducts.com.

Direct Connection R/C; distributed by Capstone R/C Suppliers, 562 W. Schrock Rd., Westerville, OH 43081; (614) 899-6313; fax (614) 899-6070.

Dremel Tool, 4915 21st St., Racine, WI 53406; (414) 554-1390; fax (414) 554-7654.

Du-Bro Products, P.O. Box 815, Wauconda, IL 60084; (800) 848-9411; fax (847) 526-1604; www.dubro.com

Estes Industries, 1295 H St., Penrose, CO 81240; (719) 372-6565; fax (719) 372-3419.

F&M Enterprises, 22522 Auburn Dr., El Toro, CA 92630; (714) 583-1455; fax (714) 583-1455.

Florio Flyer Corp., P.O. Box 88, Dagus Mines, PA 15831.

Futaba Corp. of America, P.O. Box 19767, Irvine, CA 92723-9767; (949) 455-9888; fax (949) 455-9899.

Global Hobby Distributors, 18480 Bandilier Circle, Fountain Valley, CA 92728-8610; (714) 964-0827; fax (714) 962-6452.

Graupner; distributed by Hobby Lobby Intl. (address below).

Great Planes Model Distributors, 2904 Research Rd., P.O. Box 9021, Champaign, IL 61826-9021; (800) 682-8948; fax (217) 398-0008; www.greatplanes.com

Harry Higley & Sons Inc., P.O. Box 532, Glenwood, IL 60425.

Hirobo; distributed by Model Rectifier Corp (address below).

Hitec RCD Inc., 10729 Wheatlands Ave., Ste. C, Santee, CA 92071-2854; (619) 258-4940; fax (619) 449-1002; www.hitecrcd.com

Hobbico; distributed by Great Planes (address above).

Hobby Lobby Intl., 5614 Franklin Pike Cir., Brentwood, TN 37027; (615) 373-1444; fax (615) 377-6948; www.hobby-lobby.com

Hobby Poxy, 36 Pine St., Rockaway, NJ 07866; (973) 625-3100; fax (973) 625-8303.

J&Z Products, 25029 S. Vermont Ave., Harbor City, CA 90710; (310) 539-2313.

JR, 4105 Fieldstone Rd., Champaign, IL 61821; (217) 355-9511; www.horizonhobby.com

Landing Products; distributed by APC Props (address above).

Loctite, 18731 Cranwood Ct., Cleveland, OH 44128; (216) 475-3600.

Master Airscrew; distributed by Windsor Propeller Co., 3219 Monier Cir., Rancho Cordova, CA 95742; (916) 631-8385; fax (916) 631-8386.

McDaniel R/C Inc., 1654 Crofton Blvd., Ste. 4, Crofton, MD 21114; (410) 721-6303; (301) 721-6306.

Model Airplane News; to subscribe, call (800) 827-0323 (in USA and Canada), or (815) 734-1116 elsewhere; www.modelairplanenews.com

Model Rectifier Corp. (MRC), 80 Newfield Ave., Edison, NJ 08818-6312; (732) 225-6360; fax (732) 225-0091; www.modelrec.com

MonoKote; distributed by Great Planes (address above).

Nick Ziroli Design and Engineering, 605 East Monroe St., Little Falls, NY 13365; (315) 823-1208.

Nick Ziroli Plans, 29 Edgar Dr., Smithtown, NY 11787; (516) 467-4765; fax (516) 467-1752.

O.S.; distributed by Great Planes (address above); www.osengines.com

Oracover; distributed by Hobby Lobby Intl. (address above).

Pacer Technology (mfr. of Zap adhesives) 9420 Santa Anita Ave., Rancho Cucamonga, CA 91730; (909) 987-0550; (800) 538-3091.

Performance Products Unlimited; distributed by Dave Brown Products (address above).

Robart Mfg., P.O. Box 1247, 625 N. 12th St., St. Charles, IL 60174; (630) 584-7616; fax (630) 584-3712;www.robart.com

Saito, 4105 Fieldstone Rd., Champaign, IL 61821; (217) 355-9511; www.horizonhobby.com

Sermos R/C Snap Connectors Inc., Cedar Corners Station, Box 16787, Stamford, CT 06905.

Sig Mfg. Co., 401 S. Front St., Montezuma, IA 50171; (800) 247-5008; fax (515) 623-3922.

Sport Flyers of America, P.O. Box 7993, Haledon, NJ 07508; (800) 745-3597; fax (973) 305-6686; www.modelaviation.com

Sullivan Products, P.O. Box 5166, Baltimore, MD 21224; (410) 732-3500; fax (410) 327-7443.

Thunder Tiger USA; distributed by Ace Hobby Distributors (address above).

Top Flite; distributed by Great Planes (address above).

Tower Hobbies, P.O. Box 9078, Champaign, IL 61826-9078; (800) 637-4989; fax (800) 637-7303. www.towerhobbies.com

U.S. AirCore, 4576 Claire Chennault, Hangar 7, Dallas, TX 75248; (214) 250-1914.

Webra, 4105 Fieldstone Rd., Champaign, IL 61821; (217) 355-9511; www.horizonhobby.com

Websites

Academy of Model Aeronautics (AMA) www.modelaircraft.org

E-Zone www.ezonemag.com

International Miniature Aerobatics Club (IMAC) www.mini-iac.com

International Miniature Aircraft Association (IMAA) www.fly-imaa.org

Jet Pilots Organization (JPO) www.jetpilots.org

Joe Nall Giant Scale Fly In www.hartness.com/events/nall/joenall.htm

League of Silent Flight (LSF) www.silentflight.org

Model Aeronautics Association of Canada www.maac.ca

Model Airplane News **magazine** www.modelairplanenews.com

National Association of Scale Aeromodelers (NASA) www.scaleaero.com

National Miniature Pylon Racing Association (NMPRA) www.nmpra.net/

Northeast IMAC www.mini-iac.com/Northeast/region_northeast.htm

R/C Web Directory Index www.towerhobbies.com/rcweb.html

R/C TV www.rctv1.com

Society of Antique Modelers (SAM) www.antiquemodeler.org

Southern Scale Warbird Association www.geocities.com/CapeCanaveral/9771

Sport Flyers of America www.modelaviation.com

Toledo Model Expo www.toledoshow.com

Unlimited Scale Racing Association www.usra-racers.org

W3MH (online helicopter magazine) www.lance.co.uk/w3mh

WRAM Show www.wram.org

Conversion Charts

COMMONLY USED TAP/DRILL SIZES

Screw-thread size	Use drill-bit size
2-56	.51
3-48	5/64
4-40	.43
6-32	.36
8-32	.29
10-24	.25
10-32	.21
1/4-20	.8
1/4-28	.3

DECIMAL EQUIVALENTS

1/64	0.0156
1/32	0.0313
3/64	0.0469
1/16	0.0625
5/64	0.0781
1/8	0.125
3/16	0.1875
1/4	0.25

METRIC CONVERSION CHART

Inch	mm
1/64	0.396
1/32	0.793
1/16	1.587
3/32	2.381
1/8	3.175
5/32	3.968
3/16	4.762
1/4	6.350
5/16	7.937
3/8	9.525
1/2	12.700
3/4	19.050

Before you fly

❏ Double-check the CG; is it where the instructions say it should be?

❏ Check all control surfaces for freedom of movement. Do any show signs of inappropriate slop or binding?

❏ Check all the screws, clevises, nuts and control horns. Did you forget to connect any? Are all the clevises secured with a safety clip or a short length of fuel tubing?

❏ Is the radio equipment wrapped with foam and securely positioned in the fuselage?

❏ Have you ground-checked your radio to ensure that it sends a strong signal and that your receiver is picking up control inputs?

❏ Is all the fuel tubing properly connected and free of kinks?

❏ Have you fully charged your onboard batteries? (depleted batteries are a common cause of model crashes).

❏ Is your plane properly fueled?

❏ Do any of the servo-lead wires interfere with the servo arms or the pushrods?

❏ Is the antenna properly strung and uncoiled?

❏ Do your servos respond properly to control inputs? (reversed servos are another common cause of crashes).

❏ Ground-check your radio: with the TX and receiver turned on, collapse the antenna and walk 75 feet away from your aircraft. Move the control sticks to check that the TX and RX are working properly. Extend the antenna before takeoff.

You might want to photocopy this page and keep it in your flight box.